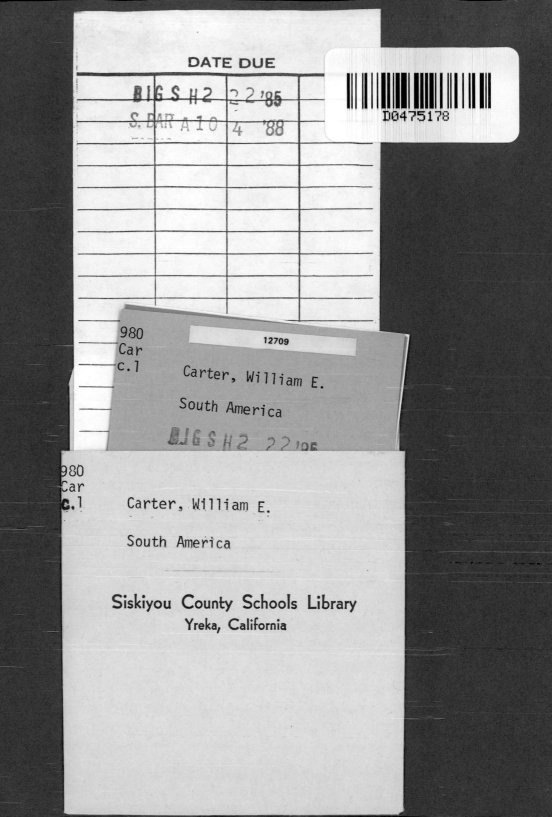

South America

South America

William E. Carter

A FIRST BOOK | REVISED EDITION
FRANKLIN WATTS
NEW YORK | LONDON | TORONTO | SYDNEY | 1983

FRONTIS: PRE-COLUMBIAN VESSEL OF
SILVER AND TURQUOISE FROM PERU

Map courtesy of Vantage Art, Inc.

Cover photograph of Payne Park, Chile,
courtesy of Taurus Photos (Janet Bennett)

Photographs courtesy of
The Metropolitan Museum of Art: opp. title page, p. 22;
United Nations: pp. 3, 65 (by J. Frank);
World Food Program/FAO:
pp. 8 (by Peyton Johnson), 25 (by F. Mattioli),
30 (by F. Mattioli), 33 (by Peyton Johnson);
United Press International: pp. 13, 60, 70, 77, 80;
Colombia Information Service: p. 16;
International Labor Office/FAO; p. 36;
Government Information Services, British Guiana: p. 45.

Library of Congress Cataloging in Publication Data

Carter, William E.
South America.

(A First book)
Rev. ed. of: The first book of South America.
Rev. ed., 2nd ed. 1972.
Includes index.
Summary: Explores the geography, history,
and civilization of the twelve nations and
one French department which constitute
the fourth largest continent.
1. South America—Juvenile literature.
[1. South America] I. Title.
F2208.5.C3 1983   980   82-17477
ISBN 0-531-04531-5

Contents

FOR MY CHILDREN
WHO WERE:

EMILY, VIVIAN,
AND OLIVIA

A Continent of Contrasts

Of the seven continents of the world, South America is the fourth in size—smaller than Asia, Africa, and North America, but larger than Europe, Antarctica, and Australia. South America contains twelve independent nations, plus one overseas department of France. Each of these political units is a world unto itself. Each has its own particular type of climate and landscape, each has its own special kind of population, each has its own way of doing things, and each is proud of its individuality and independence.

The main reason the nations of South America differ so much from one another is that most of them began, just after America was discovered by Europeans, as an isolated cluster of either Spanish- or Portuguese-speaking people who settled in places where they thought they had a good chance of getting rich quickly. These settlement clusters were far apart, and tended to be separated by great natural barriers such as mountains, dense forests, jungles, and deserts. As a result, over the years, each cluster grew in its own way and became different from all the others. So it was that when South Americans began to free themselves from Spain and Portugal in the early years of the nineteenth century, from these isolated settlement clusters came separate nations.

Look at a large map and you will see that even today very few railways and highways connect one South American nation with another. The last links of the Pan American highway have just been completed. For the first time in history roads have been opened into the heart of the Amazon basin, and an important road has been projected that will run north and south, down the entire eastern slopes of the Andes.

South America is a continent of contrasts and surprises. Much of its land is empty, yet its population is growing faster than that of even Asia. It continues to have many backward, isolated, and poor areas, and yet many of its cities are large, beautiful, and modern. Its two main languages, Spanish and Portuguese, are European, and yet its people have come from every corner of the world.

The first people to arrive were the Indians. They were given this name by Columbus, for when he discovered America in 1492, he thought he had landed in the East Indies.

Contrary to what many people believe, South American Indians are not one people, but many different ones. Yet all of them seem to be descended from Asians who, between ten and thirty thousand years ago, crossed over where the Bering Strait now separates Alaska from the Soviet Union. These people may have come to the American continents by one of a number of ways: by land, by ice, by water, or by island-hopping—no one is certain.

Gradually these first immigrants spread from north to south and west to east. By 8000 B.C., they were living even at the southernmost tip of the continent. They reached this spot because their ancestors had walked great distances in search of wild game and food plants. Once the continent was pretty much settled, little by

The fortress city of Machu Picchu,
an engineering marvel of the Inca
empire, was carved into a mountain
ridge 2,000 feet (606 m) above
the Urabamba River in Peru.

little some of these Indians tried to domesticate the game and improve and harvest the plants. Those who succeeded were able to stop roaming, settle down, and build towns. Over the centuries a number of these towns grew and, by banding together, developed into chiefdoms and even empires.

Following Columbus's discovery, the Spaniards and the Portuguese were the two main groups of white men to explore and settle the land. In 1493 Pope Alexander VI drew a line on a map of the New World, assigning everything west of the line to the Spaniards and everything east of the line to the Portuguese. Though no one realized it at the time, this division gave all the west coast and most of the interior of South America to the Spaniards, and only a piece of the east coast to the Portuguese. Once the Portuguese discovered what had happened, they were displeased. So it was that, as settlement began in earnest, Portuguese explorers expanded into the entire heart of the continent and set the base for the immense territory known today as Brazil.

Both the Spaniards and the Portuguese came from a part of Europe known as the Iberian Peninsula. There they were used to a system of great estates, over each of which there was a lord or *patrón (patrão* in Portuguese), and to a similar system of privilege for leaders of the Church and the armed forces. This meant that their societies were made up of people of two basic types: aristocrats who were the lords, knights, priests, and military officials, and commoners who were the serfs, manual laborers, and ordinary soldiers and sailors.

The Spanish and Portuguese colonists tried to imitate this system when they opened the newly discovered lands of South America. But they all wanted to be aristocrats; no one who could avoid it wanted to be a commoner. Many of the Spaniards, even the poor ones, found this ideal easy to achieve. On the west coast were the Inca Empire and the Chibcha chiefdoms. Each of these contained large numbers of Indians who were used to long, hard hours of labor, and to taking orders from lords and princes. If a little force was used, they could be made to work just as hard for their new masters. So it was here that the Spaniards built their first large settlements, in lands that today are divided into several Andean

—4—

nations: Colombia, Ecuador, Peru, Bolivia, and the northwestern part of Argentina.

The Portuguese were not so fortunate. In the land marked for them by Pope Alexander there were no great nations or empires. Instead, there were only scattered towns, each one independent from the others. The Indians in this part of South America were used to making only small clearings in the tropical forest, where they planted their main crops—squash, beans, and a starchy root called manioc. They were not in the habit of working long and hard hours under the orders of lords and princes.

Early Spanish settlers in the Andes were fortunate not only in finding a good labor force; they also discovered large deposits of gold and silver. The early Portuguese found nothing like this in the lands assigned to them. How were they to make use of their part of the continent? To do anything at all, they badly needed labor. Yet most of the Indians they met refused to work, ran away, or grew sick and died.

To solve their problem, they began to import black slaves from Africa. Soon the northeastern coast of South America, in the area that is now Brazil, had the richest sugar plantations in the world. Pleased with how well these first slaves worked, the Portuguese imported more and more, until this part of South America had many more blacks than whites.

In certain parts of the continent assigned to the Spaniards, similar developments took place. Large sections of the northern and western coasts were empty, for most of the people of the great Indian chiefdoms and empires lived in the mountains. To produce coastal crops and carry on trade in these areas, the Spaniards brought in blacks from Africa. As a result, many of the people who now live in Venezuela and Colombia have some African ancestry.

Southwest of the Portuguese part of South America, early settlers found one of the wildest and loneliest parts of the continent. On the north it was known as the *pampa*, the Indian word for "flatland," and on the south as *Patagonia*, or "Big Feet," because of the huge size of footprints the early explorers found there. The Indians who were native to these two areas were very primitive and lived in small, roving bands that depended almost entirely on what they could hunt. Two of their favorite foods were the South American ostrich and the guanaco.

Though ostriches are well known to North Americans, guanacos are not nearly so familiar. They are about the size of donkeys, are very swift, and are distantly related to the camel. Because the Indians of South America did not have horses, they had to hunt on foot. For guanacos and ostriches, their best weapon was the *boleador*, three long strips of rawhide with a stone ball tied to the outer end of each strip. By throwing this weapon at a running guanaco or ostrich, a hunter could easily tangle the rawhide strips around the animal's legs, even though it was fleeing at full speed.

Hunters who live from game that they chase by foot can seldom settle down, build towns, and accumulate wealth. So it was that when the Spaniards first came to the *pampas* and Patagonia, they found that the natives were poor and scattered. When the Spaniards also found that the region contained neither silver nor gold, their interest shifted quickly to other places. The result was that, until the nineteenth century, this part of South America was nearly forgotten. Then people discovered that the grasslands over which the guanacos had roamed were perfect for raising great herds of cattle and sheep, and the region began to grow.

Spaniards, Italians, French, Swiss, Germans, English, Danes, Russians, and Welshmen came and built farms, towns, and cities like the ones they had known in Europe. The few Indians who had lived in the region died out, were killed, or intermarried with the descendants of the old Spanish settlers and with the newcomers. In this part of South America today almost everyone is white, and people live in much the same way they do in Europe.

Not all Europeans who migrated to South America during the past century went to the *pampas*, of course. Large numbers of Germans went to southern Chile and southern Brazil, where their descendants continue to be blond haired and blue eyed. Many of the houses of the German region of southern Chile look like the houses of the Black Forest of Germany. So beautiful is the area that it has been called the Switzerland of South America, and today it is a major center for tourists and sports fishermen.

People from even more distant parts of the world now call South America their home. There is a colony of settlers from Java who have lived for several generations in Surinam. There are large groups of Japanese farmers in the interior of Brazil. In Lima, Peru, there is a sizable colony of Chinese. And in eastern Bolivia there are colonists from Okinawa, an island in the Pacific Ocean.

Today the populations of Ecuador, Peru, and Bolivia continue to be mostly Indian by race. In Colombia, Venezuela, Chile, and Paraguay, large numbers of the people are *mestizos*—part Indian and part Spanish. Blacks occupy important sections of the coasts of Venezuela and Colombia. In Brazil, great numbers of people come from a mixture of three different racial groups—black, white, and Indian. And in Uruguay and Argentina nearly everyone is white.

One reason South America has appealed to so many different kinds of people is the continent's great variety of climates. In some places there is always ice and snow. In others there is either perpetual summer or perpetual spring. And in still others there are great contrasts from one season to the next.

In those parts of South America that lie south of the equator—that is, on most of the continent—seasons are the reverse of what they are in Europe and North America. Christmas comes in summer, Easter comes in the fall, and the shortest day of the year comes in June.

Where the equator stretches across northern South America, the sun's rays shine directly down and carry great heat. Because the Amazon Valley lies almost at sea level and is either on or near the equator, it has a lowland tropical climate—summer weather the year round. Quito, Ecuador, which also lies very near the equator but nearly 2 miles (3.2. km) above sea level, has delightful, springlike weather the year round. And the mountaintops near Quito, though some lie directly on the equator, are covered with deep, eternal snows.

The Andes are the second highest chain of mountains in the world; only the Himalayas of Asia are higher. Forming the backbone of South America, the Andes rise out of the Caribbean Sea and continue southward for more than 4,000 miles (6,400 km) until

*Although near the equator in Ecuador,
the volcano Cotopaxi is snow-capped
the year round because of its altitude.*

they dive into the ocean waters at Tierra del Fuego, the southernmost tip of the continent. Varying from 20 to more than 500 miles (32 to 800 km) in width, they climb in places to more than four miles (6.4 km) in height. The highest peak, Mount Aconcagua, on the Argentine border with Chile, is nearly 23,000 feet (6,900 m) high.

The enormous height of the Andes cuts the whole eastern part of the continent off from the western part. Clouds coming in from the Atlantic Ocean cool as they climb over the rising land, and their moisture turns to rain on the *east* side of the mountains. In contrast, on much of the *west* side, the clouds that rise from the Pacific absorb rather than lose moisture. This is due to the coldness and swiftness of the Humboldt Current, a wide, deep stream of water that sweeps up the Pacific Coast from the Antarctic Ocean. To the far south, where the land is still cool, generous amounts of rain fall as the clouds coming off the Humboldt Current are cooled even more by the frigid land. So it is that southern Chile has about 200 inches (508 cm) of rainfall a year. But as the current moves northward it runs along ever warmer land. As the ocean clouds move over this land, they absorb rather than drop moisture. As a result, the driest desert in the world, the Atacama, stretches along the Pacific coast for 2,000 miles (3,200 km)—in some places to a width of 200 miles (320 km). Throughout much of this desert there is an average of only 1 inch (2.54 cm) of rain every seven years, and one weather station has recorded no rainfall at all in nearly one hundred years.

As if purposely to make South America a land of contrasts, another current—the Equatorial—flows southward from the northwestern shoulder of the continent. As its damp, warm air blows over the cooler land of the nearby coast, its moisture turns to drenching rain. Places like Buenaventura, Colombia, receive as much a 350 inches (889) cm) of rainfall each year.

We see, then, that the very same region of South America, its Pacific coast, has both the wettest and the driest lands on earth. And it has these because of the simple action of two giant ocean currents—the Humboldt and the Equatorial.

In spite of the continent's many contrasts, South American nations have many things in common. Most of their people are Roman Catholic in religion, most speak Spanish or Portuguese, and most believe strongly in the future of their countries. Except for French Guiana, every nation is a republic modeled after the idea of a democracy, and in the constitution of nearly every republic may be found ideas taken from the Constitution of the United States. In all South American nations, people celebrate a whole series of colorful fiestas each year, and many of these fiestas are related in some way to the Church. Though each nation has its own special music and dances, nearly all South Americans love to listen to music and to dance. And all over the continent, soccer— *futbol*— is the most popular sport.

Where the Andes Begin

Venezuela and Colombia

VENEZUELA

At the top of South America lies Venezuela, birthplace of Simón Bolívar, the general who freed five of the South American nations from Spanish rule.

There are really four Venezuelas. The first is high in the Andes, and the second lies just west of these mountains and centers around a large body of water, Lake Maracaibo. Though the majority of Venezuelans live in these two parts of the country, together they make up only one-fourth of the nation's territory.

The third Venezuela is much larger than either of the first two. It consists of enormous plains that stretch from the Andes to the banks of the Orinoco, the third greatest river in South America. Because these plains border much of the length of the river, they are called the Orinoco Plains.

From the Orinoco River to the borders of Brazil and Guyana stretches the fourth Venezuela. Because it is made up of hills, little mountains, and plateaus, and because it borders on what was formerly British Guiana, it is known as the Guiana Highlands. This area is truly immense, covering more than half the entire country, yet relatively few people live here.

When the Spaniards first arrived in what is now Venezuela, they found that the most energetic Indians lived in the fertile valleys of the Andes, where the soil was excellent for agriculture and there was abundant but not excessive rainfall. Of the valleys near the coast, the richest was Valencia. Here the Spaniards built their first great estates. But Valencia was so low in altitude and so filled with malarial mosquitoes that the inhabitants often fell victim to the disease. Because of this, many of the estate owners, looking for a more healthful climate, moved to Caracas, the city that eventually became the country's capital.

The valley of Caracas lies about 3,000 feet (900 m) above sea level—higher than the malarial region but easy to reach, since only 6 miles (9.6 km) separate the valley from the sea. People who settled there could be close to the ships from Spain and at the same time enjoy a healthful mountain climate.

From its beginnings, Caracas has been a city of aristocrats. And from its beginnings it has been the center for most of the political and economic affairs of the country. Today it has some three million people, though it grew to this size only recently. As late as 1940 it had less than one-tenth its present population—about two hundred thousand. The reason for its quick growth can be explained by the discovery of the country's black gold: oil.

The center of Venezuela's oil production is Lake Maracaibo. When the early explorers first came upon this region, they found Indians living in small houses built on pilings over the lake's waters. Looking at the way the houses were built right over the water, some of the explorers were reminded of the canals of Venice, and so they called the new country "Little Venice," or Venezuela.

For centuries Indian fishermen living on the lake must have wondered about the annoying black substance that gummed up their fishing nets. Only in this century, when experts began to arrive from England, the United States, and the Netherlands, did the real wealth of that black, gummy substance become known.

This wealth has brought amazing changes to Venezuela. Before 1918 the town of Maracaibo was sleepy and tiny. Today it is

*Oil derricks on Venezuela's Lake Maracaibo,
the largest oil field in South America*

a modern city of more than six hundred thousand people. It has huge supermarkets, hospitals, churches, and block upon block of beautiful homes. Its streets are lined with shiny automobiles. Since 1930, because of Maracaibo's oil fields, Venezuela has held a major place in world oil production. Only the Arab countries, the Soviet Union, and the United States have regularly produced more.

When Venezuelans saw how much wealth was coming into their country because of their oil production, they began to fill Caracas, their capital city, with luxury. First of all, a new highway was built to connect the city with its Caribbean port, La Guaira. Before completion of the highway, and in spite of the fact that Caracas and La Guaira were only 6 miles (9.6 km) apart, a car going between the two cities had to travel 21 miles (33.6 km) and climb up over a pass 3,400 feet (1,020 m) high. With the new road, the trip was shortened so much that it now takes only fifteen minutes.

People who travel to Caracas today are impressed by the number of skyscrapers, the quantity of luxury goods of all types, and the amount of money handled by many of the residents. But they are also struck by the masses of poor people whose makeshift houses line the mountainsides.

A number of years ago, in an attempt to distribute the wealth better and to prepare for the time when the oil will run out, the Venezuelan government began to use its oil money to create other industries. So successful has this program been that today the government controls 40 percent of the means of production and produces half of the gross national product. But it is finding that many problems still need to be solved. The industries it has built are so modern that they require very few workers, or workers so skilled that they are in short supply. Rather than provide a profit, many government industries regularly lose money. The steel industry is a good example. One of the richest iron deposits in the world is that of Cerro Bolívar, in the Guiana Highlands. The Venezuelan government thought that by using this iron to create a steel industry, the country would have a new source of wealth. Instead, it now finds that, by producing steel, it is losing as much as one million dollars a day.

Venezuela's experience is that wealth can create as well as solve problems. It still has the problem of many poor people, and of

—14—

many people who want to work but cannot find a job. Its leaders see that some things can be done better by private individuals than by government, and that great care must be taken so that, from the oil, the country can have new sources of wealth rather than new problems. Much of this new wealth they expect to come from the Orinoco Plains and the Guiana Highlands. They know that part of the year the plains have too much rainfall and part of the year not enough. But Venezuelan engineers have now learned how to control the water so that the plains can be irrigated, and fine cattle and rice can be produced there. Venezuela's leaders know that the Guiana Highlands have huge deposits of both iron ore, which is now being used to make steel, and bauxite, which is now being used to make aluminum.

Eastern Venezuela—the Orinoco Plains and the Guiana Highlands—is still in many ways a frontier. While it becomes better known each year, it remains a box of surprises not yet fully opened.

COLOMBIA

The dream of Simón Bolívar, the great leader of South American independence, was to make a single nation of what eventually became three separate ones: Venezuela, Colombia, and Ecuador. In his attempt to make his dream come true, he established the Confederation of Gran Colombia. The confederation lasted less than ten years; by 1830 both Venezuela and Ecuador had decided to go their separate ways, and even Colombia was having problems holding itself together.

Colombia, often described as a collection of diverse peoples and regions all in search of a nation, is a land of tremendous contrasts: desert coasts, chilly upland valleys, dense forests, coastal swamps, snowcapped mountains, and flood-swollen Amazon rivers. The most contrasts of all are found in the western third of the country. Here, where most Colombians live, the Andes break into three separate mountain chains and so fragment the landscape that even neighboring valleys look as if they belong to different countries. The climate and terrain are so varied that nearly three thousand different species of birds inhabit the region.

*Many new, modern buildings are prominent
in Bogotá, the capital of Colombia.*

For many centuries before the Spanish conquest, Colombia was home to two major groups of people: the Chibcha, who lived in the high Andes, and the Carib, who lived in the valleys and along the coasts. Next to the Incas of Peru and Bolivia, the Chibcha were the most advanced society in South America. They had a complex political structure, a tax system, temples, aqueducts, roads, bridges, and complex agriculture. For thousands of years their ancestors had grown cotton, potatoes, yucca, beans, and corn. Long before the Spanish conquest, they were producing enough surplus to support chiefs and priests in luxury.

The tribes of Colombia traded for, produced, and used huge quantities of gold. Much of this can be seen today in Bogotá, where a unique gold museum holds some fifteen thousand pieces, almost eight times the number of such objects in all other gold museums of the world put together. The Spaniards, always fascinated by gold, had heard of a "golden king" during some of their first explorations of Colombian territory. The story had to do with a ceremony periodically held at a lake called Guatavita. At that lake, one of the great chiefs of the Chibcha would be stripped, covered with gold dust, and submerged in the waters of the lake, leaving the dust behind as an offering to the mother earth.

Though it was tales of gold that first drew the Spaniards into the land of the Chibchas, it was the good earth and the hard work of the Indians that kept them there. At first they were disappointed to learn that the Chibcha mined more salt than gold, and that most of the precious metal came through trade. But they discovered that the fine climate and rich soil of the Chibcha land could be used to build great estates, and that Chibcha workmen were excellent. So in the middle of Chibcha land they began to build Bogotá, today a city of more than four million people, capital of a nation that contains around 30 million people and that is one of the fastest growing countries in the world.

With such rapid growth, Colombia shows newness and modernity on every hand. Every major Colombian city is sprouting skyscrapers as if they were mushrooms. But so rich is the nation's past that it can hardly be forgotten. In addition to thousands of colonial buildings, there are dozens of important archaeological sites. The largest, filled with stone carvings, is the 60-mile (96-km) long San Agustín park—so huge that many travel through it on horseback.

Although coffee continues to be Colombia's main source of foreign exchange, and emeralds continue to be one of its best-known exports, new industries, such as flower growing and tourism, are becoming increasingly important. Carnations, chrysanthemums, roses, and other flowers are flown regularly to markets in Miami and New York, and tourists from all over the world arrive just as regularly at one of the country's great airports. Two things many insist on seeing are the Salt Cathedral and the town of Guatavita. The cathedral is a huge church carved out of the chambers of an underground salt mine by the miners themselves. And the town of Guatavita is a picture-postcard imitation of a colonial town, designed by modern architects to replace the original town of Guatavita that was flooded because of the construction of a dam.

If Bogotá is Colombia's political center, Medellín is its industrial center. Lying about 5,000 feet (1,500 m) above sea level, Medellín is the capital of Antioquia, a region that in colonial days was famous for gold mining. For years the miners of Antioquia spent enormous sums for food, which was brought in at great cost from other parts of the country. Because all of the region's food had to be imported, the region did not progress until Antonio Mon y Velarde, a Spanish officer, ordered everyone who was not a miner to plant maize, or Indian corn. Then he ordered the planters to use the corn to feed hogs and chickens, and to sell these to the miners. Finally he obtained permission from the king of Spain to divide certain lands into small farms to be worked by the owners themselves, quite different from what was happening on the great estates around Bogotá.

From that time onward, the people of Antioquia have been hardworking and industrious. When, in the last century, coffee was brought to the country, they were among the first to plant it, and when, in this century, modern industry came, they were among the first to take advantage of it. Today, though not alone, they are leaders in making Colombia one of the great industrial powers of South America.

Far south of Medellín, in a low valley between the western and

—18—

central chains of the Andes, lies Colombia's third largest city, Cali. Like Medellín, it has more than one million people. But the histories of the two cities are very different, for Cali has been a center for great sugar plantations and cattle ranches since colonial days.

Because the valley around Cali is low and mosquitoes can breed there, the early inhabitants often had malaria. To escape the disease, many plantation owners moved to Popayán—farther south and much higher up in the valley—just as the Valencian estate owners of Venezuela had moved to Caracas. But Caracas has become a great capital of more than three million people, while Popayán, in spite of its long history and wealth, is still a small city. Because it has stayed small and was for so many years the home of aristocrats, Popayán keeps alive today old Spanish traditions forgotten elsewhere. Like many Colombians, its people are fervently religious. Their celebration of Holy Week draws pilgrims from all over the country. When the pilgrims go to Popayán, one place they love to stay is an old monastery converted into a hotel and restaurant that is a living reminder of the city's beautiful and peaceful past.

Even more important as a living museum than Popayán is the northern coastal city of Cartagena. There one can see the church where Saint Peter Clavier ministered to newly arrived African slaves, the palace that housed the hated Inquisition, and the enormous fort and city wall that were built to protect the city from English pirates.

Nearly every Colombian city has its own special festivities. In Barranquilla, an important port on the Caribbean Sea, a brilliant, noisy carnival is held during the week preceding Ash Wednesday. And every June, in Buenaventura, the main Pacific Coast port, fortunes are told by the shape an egg takes when it is broken into a glass of water. If, after twelve hours, it looks like a chicken, the person seeking his fortune can expect to have a farm; if it looks like a ship, he will travel; if it looks like a tomb, he is going to die.

Over the past few decades, Colombians have tried very hard to bring the many contrasting parts of their country closer together. In many ways they have succeeded. Colombia today has fewer contrasts than before, but it is still a nation of incredible variety.

Lands of the Inca

Ecuador, Peru, and Bolivia

In 1532, when the Spaniards reached the west coast of South America, they found an Indian empire that stretched almost 3,000 miles (4,800 km) along the Pacific coast and up and down the Andes. Because the ruler of this empire was called Inca, the Spaniards gave that name to everyone living in his lands.

As a people, the Incas were not very ancient. None of their cities had existed four hundred years before the Spanish conquest, and the expansion of their empire dated only from the fifteenth century. They were able to accomplish as much as they did mainly because of all the great civilizations that had gone before them.

One of the finest of these was the Mochica. This civilization developed in irrigated desert valleys on the northern coast of Peru a little more than two thousand years ago, just before the time of Christ. The largest structure it left is today known as the Temple of the Sun. To build it the Mochica had to gather together 130 million mud bricks.

We know more about the Mochica than about most ancient peoples because they loved to make pots, with decorations showing how all sorts of people lived. By using molds, they manufactured hundreds at a time. They made pots representing dogs, llamas, fishermen, warriors, farmers, priests, physicians, sweethearts, mothers, babies, sick people—in fact, just about anything in life. Some of the pots seem to have been made for fun and have two pipelike openings leading out a hollow, curved handle attached to their back. When water is poured out of one of the openings, the other whistles.

The Mochica were by no means alone in developing high culture. The Peruvian coast gave rise to many great, early civilizations. To the south, in the desert dryness of the Atacama, the people of one of these civilizations built geometric patterns by heaping up low ridges of stones and earth. So extensive are these ridges that their design can be seen only from the air. No one knows why they were made or by whom.

The same coastal desert was home to the people of Paracas, some of the finest weavers who ever lived. We know a great deal about their art because of the discovery of a large tomb where 429 mummies were found, wrapped in yards and yards of cloth and even provided with changes of clothing. Each mummy bundle was protected by a layer of clay. Because of this protection, and because of the dry desert air, much of the cloth and clothing is still in perfect condition. There is gauze, doubled-faced weaving (cloth that looks exactly the same on both sides), and whole wardrobes of intricate, brilliantly colored design. Much of the weaving is overlaid with embroidery, the finest of which was made with fish bone needles so thin as to be transparent. All this may be seen today in museums in Lima, Peru's capital city.

Cloth has for centuries been the main art form of the Andean Indians. Even stone carvers have taken it as a model. So it was with the stone carvers of Tiahuanacu, a major temple center for yet another early civilization, located high in the Andes along the shores of Lake Titicaca. Since the figures they carved are copies of woven designs, they look squarish, as if they had come off a loom rather than out of stone.

The cloth model was even used for mud-brick construction. A prime example is the pre-Inca city of Chan Chan, on the northern

The skill of the early Indian weavers
is evident in this Peruvian mantle,
embroidered over five hundred years ago.

coast of Peru. Walls in that city, though of dried mud, take on the pattern of fine lace.

Though conquered by the Incas, great Andean civilizations such as Chan Chan provided a solid base for the new empire. At first no one suspected that this could happen. The Incas had been a small, unimportant group living near the mountain town of Cuzco. They never became as good potters as the Mochica, as good weavers as the people of Nazca, as good stone carvers as the people of Tiahuanacu, or as good builders of adobe as the people of Chan Chan. But they did become determined rulers, and once they got their empire started it grew swiftly.

The head Inca was absolute dictator and, by law, owner of all lands. Yet he saw to it that each family had its plots to till, and that most were assigned the same plots generation after generation. If his subjects rebelled, he would have them moved to a different part of the empire, and would replace them with others who were more loyal. If a family line died out, he would order that the plots they had used be given to another household.

Though the Incas had neither wheeled vehicles nor horses, roads connected every part of their empire. Royal runners were hired to carry messages, treasure, and even special food for the Inca's table from every corner of the land. On one and the same day the ruler could enjoy fish from the sea, potatoes from the mountains, and fruit from the jungle.

Storehouses were scattered everywhere and were drawn upon to avoid famine and to feed the nobles, priests, soldiers, and even the common man when in the service of his lord. Roads, irrigation works, and terraces built with such labor were so fine that many are still used today.

When the Spanish conqueror, Francisco Pizarro, arrived in Peru in 1532, he had fewer than two hundred soldiers. The Inca, commanding an empire of more than ten million and thinking that Pizarro might be a god, ordered him treated as an honored guest. His reward was to be imprisoned by the Spaniard and held for ransom. Gold to ransom the Inca flooded in from all quarters of the empire—some say fifteen million dollars worth—but once Pizarro got his hands on it, he accused the Inca of having killed his brother, tried him, and ordered him put to death. With their great ruler dead, most of the Indians, feeling helpless and confused, simply gave in to the Spaniards.

Today the core lands of the Incas form the heartlands of three independent countries: Ecuador, Peru, and Bolivia.

ECUADOR

Quito was the first name given this land by the Spanish conquerors, for it was home to the Quitus Indians. Only after a French expedition in the late eighteenth century proved that the territory straddled the northern and southern hemispheres did it begin to be known as Ecuador, land of the equator.

The word Quito remains, however, in the name of the capital city. Twelve miles (19.2 km) north of this city, in the little village of San Antonio, the traveler can stand with one foot in the northern and the other in the southern half of our planet. Only a monument and a tourist center mark the spot, for the dividing point itself is, of course, invisible.

Though Ecuador sits astride the equator, its climate is surprisingly pleasant. The great height of the Andes cools the mountain valleys, and the immense cold mass of the Humboldt Current tempers much of the coast. Because the country lies on or near the equator, there is no real summer or winter, but only a dry season and a wet one.

Partly because the mountain valleys have such delicious, spring-like climate the year round, about half of Ecuador's population lives there. The capitol, Quito, is the largest mountain city. It is very old, and just before the Spanish conquest, served as capital of the Incas' northern empire. After the conquest it became a treasure house of art and culture and is filled even today with beautifully decorated churches and palaces, preserved from that early period.

Most of the people who live in the highlands today have both Indian and Spanish ancestry. Their craftsmen have made a unique blend of the art of both traditions. They work with many materials and techniques: wood, stone, clay, weaving and embroidery. Some of the most unusual of their products are little dolls made out of

*Cereals on sale in an open-air
market held weekly at Otavalo*

bread dough. Originally used only for religious celebrations, today these dolls have found their way into tourist markets and even museums. They represent people from all levels of society; animals such as chickens, dogs, and horses; and even inanimate objects such as houses and automobiles. Brightly colored, finely detailed, and highly varnished, they can be kept and admired for years.

Much of the coast, the second major region of Ecuador, is covered with lush jungle. Toward the south, however, where the cool Humboldt Current sweeps up from Peru, the land is dry and covered with cactus.

Most of Ecuador's export products come from this coastal region. Three of these, coffee, bananas, and cacao—the basis of chocolate—come from trees. The coastal region also produces the *tagua*, or ivory nut palm, and the balsa tree. The ivory from the *tagua* nut is used to make poker chips, chessmen, umbrella handles, and buttons. Much of the very light and soft wood from the balsa tree ends up as model airplanes and toys.

The chief city of the coast, and the largest city in Ecuador today, is Guayaquil. When Guayaquil was smaller, cacao and coffee beans were laid out on its streets to dry. Today these same streets are choked with traffic, for Guayaquil has become the business capital of the country. It is also Ecuador's major port, in spite of the fact that it lies 40 miles (64 km) upriver from the point where the Guayas flows into the Pacific.

The greatest writers of modern Ecuador either were born in Guayaquil or for many years lived in that city. Their novels have become models for writers working not only in other South American countries, but even in the United States and Europe. In their books, they play with time and thought, jumping back and forth among the present, past, and future, and entering the world of the mind.

Ecuador's third major region is part of the Amazon basin, lies east of the Andes, and is sparsely populated. Most of the few people who have traditionally lived there are tribal Indians. The two best-known groups are the Jívaro and the Colorados. In the past the Jívaro were fierce warriors, beheading their conquered enemies and shrinking their heads to the size of oranges. Their principal weapons were poison darts shot from blowguns. Visitors to the area can still buy "shrunken heads" from the Jívaro, but these heads are now made out of goatskin or plastic.

The Colorados are a peaceful group, known above all for the unusual way in which they adorn themselves. For festive occasions, red and black stripes are painted across the bodies and faces of men, women, and children alike, and men rub thick red dye into their hair until it looks like a rusty, stiff helmet.

Groups such as the Jívaro and Colorado are being swept into modern life by the opening of Ecuador's Amazonian frontier. The discovery of oil on the eastern slopes of the Andes has helped the Ecuadorian economy, but it has meant that the region will never again be the same. Many sons and daughters of tribal Indians have now moved to cities like Quito and some earn college degrees.

Ecuador's fourth main region, the Galápagos Islands, lies astride the equator, some 600 miles (960 km) west of the Pacific coast. In Spanish, *galápagos* means "tortoises," a name given to the islands because of the huge land turtles the discoverers found there. Some of these giants weighed more than 500 pounds (225 kg).

In 1835, when he was only twenty-six, the famous naturalist Charles Darwin visited the Galápagos. He noticed that the animals on the islands were different from any he had seen anywhere else and that they differed slightly from one island to another. Could it be possible, Darwin wondered, that these living creatures were changing to fit special conditions on the islands? Could it be that they were on their way to becoming new species?

Many years later, Charles Darwin startled the world when in his great book, *The Origin of Species*, he gave his answer as, Yes. The Galápagos Islands had given him the key to his famous theory of evolution; the theory states that various kinds of plants and animals now in existence have slowly developed from previously existing kinds.

PERU

Like most other countries of the Andes, Peru is divided into coast, mountain, and jungle. Because of the cool waters of the Humboldt

Current, the coast is very dry, averaging less than 2 inches (5.08 cm) of rainfall per year. As the coastal clouds climb the Andean peaks, however, they drop their moisture first in the form of rain and then of snow. This feeds fifty-two little rivers that rush westward to the ocean and that provide water for irrigated crops and for the water supplies of cities and towns.

In the center of this desert coast lies the country's largest city and capital, Lima. Francisco Pizarro chose the site in 1535 because it bordered a river that never dried up even though rain might not fall in the area for many years. It also lay opposite several small islands that could protect anchored ships from the rough waves of the Pacific. The Incas had called the river Rimac, and it is probably from a corruption of that name that the new city came to be known as Lima.

Everywhere a person goes in Lima, he or she is reminded of history. In the enormous main plaza, on the steps of the ancient cathedral, stands a statue of Pizarro himself, and in a chapel within the cathedral a glass casket holds the great conqueror's mummy.

For much of the colonial period, Pizarro's city was the capital and most important city of the whole southern half of Spanish South America. It was filled with sprawling mansions and richly dressed men and women, and it came to be known as the continent's principal center for education and culture.

Although some of the finest of Lima's colonial buildings have been destroyed by earthquakes, far more have been torn down by developers. The city today is a vibrant place with dozens of sky-scrapers, mile after mile of factories, freeways, boulevards, villas, oceanside parks, and even slums. It seldom rains, yet the sun may not shine for weeks at a time, for fog covers most of the Peruvian coast from May to October. When rain does fall, it can bring disaster, for many houses, especially of the poor, have been built to withstand only dry weather. The worst of the area's rare rainstorms tend to come around Christmastime and are known as *El Niño* ("The Child"), in honor of the baby Jesus.

Moving from the coast into the mountains, a traveler enters a different world. The farther one goes, the more Indians one sees. And the higher one climbs, the harder it is to breathe, for the air in the mountains contains much less oxygen than does the air at sea level. Here, in the interior of Peru and the western part of neighboring Bolivia, are located the highest towns and cities of the world. Many travelers to this part of South America suffer from a mountain sickness known as *soroche*. Caused by a lack of oxygen, *soroche* usually lasts only a few hours or days, but it can make a person dizzy and cause splitting headaches and an upset stomach.

Cuzco, the old capital of the Inca Empire, lies at the heart of these Peruvian highlands. Many of the Indians who live in and around Cuzco still speak Quechua, the language of the Incas, and dress in costumes that blend colonial Spanish and Inca styles. When the Spaniards took over the city, they destroyed some of the Inca buildings and built on top of others. Even today there are whole city blocks where the first story of two- and three-story buildings is made out of Inca stonework and the upper stories out of Spanish adobe. Some of the stones are as big as a house and may weigh as much as two hundred tons. Scientists are still perplexed as to how Inca workers moved the stones and fitted them together, for they had neither machines nor work animals. Yet the stones are so close together that in many places the blade of a pocket knife cannot be forced between them. Even without mortar, they have resisted earthquakes that have brought the Spanish-built upper floors crashing to the ground.

Throughout the highlands, llamas and alpacas are common. Both, like the guanaco of the southern Andes, are distantly related to the Old World camel. They are not as large as horses and are too weak for people to ride. Llamas, however, can carry small burdens for long distances, and the wool of both animals is excellent for weaving. Indian herders love these animals and treat them almost as members of the family.

North and east of the Andes lies the jungle region of Peru. Here the soil is very rich, but roads are few and poor. With good roads, this region could become a breadbasket for Peru's growing population. Its greatest problem now is how to get the goods to market.

The most important city in this jungle region is Iquitos, located at the headwaters of the Amazon, 2,300 miles (3,680 km) from the

*The loads these llamas are carrying
will be used to thatch roofs.*

Atlantic Ocean. For generations, if people wanted to travel from this city to Lima, they had to go by ship down the Amazon to the Atlantic, around the southern tip of South America, and up the west coast to the Peruvian capital—a journey of many weeks. Today the two cities are joined by a modern air transport system.

The history of Peru is one of repeated swings between great wealth and great poverty. Although, in its early colonial period, immense fortunes had been made with gold and silver, by the time of independence, in 1821, these precious metals had become so scarce that the first years of the new republic were difficult ones. Then the world discovered the importance of fertilizer, and Peru began to export both guano and nitrate.

Guano was nothing more than huge mounds of droppings left by sea birds that had nested for centuries on islands just off the Peruvian coast. Before the Spanish conquest, the Indians of Peru had known the value of these droppings and had used them to fertilize their crops. But the importance of fertilizer was forgotten during the Spanish colonial period. By the time it was rediscovered, so much guano had accumulated on the sea islands that people began to mine it with large equipment and even with dynamite. They acted as if it never could be used up. But they were wrong; to protect the guano supply the government had to step in and restrict mining. Today a carefully controlled population of some two thousand workers lives on the islands, protects the birds, and collects their droppings.

Nitrate was a mineral lying on the surface of the desert, rich in nitrogen and never washed into the soil because of the lack of rain. It was much more abundant than guano, and so, until the invention of artificial nitrate, it also provided a basis for great fortunes.

More important than either guano or nitrate today is the fishing industry. By working the incredibly rich waters of the Humboldt Current, Peru has become the most important fishing nation in the world. From the fish it makes fish meal and fish meal fertilizer. Partly because of the importance of fishing to its economy, Peru lays claim to the Pacific up to 200 miles (320 km) from shore. This claim conflicts with laws of countries like the United States and has led to occasional confrontation.

—31—

One of Peru's problems has been how to distribute its great wealth more equally. Some of the richest and some of the poorest people in all South America live within its borders. Dozens of new industries have been started to increase production and give jobs to more people. A land reform has been imposed so that the rural poor can have a better chance. But many of the rich do not want to lose their privileges, and among the poor the population is growing so fast that it is almost impossible to improve food, clothing, and housing for them all. The challenge facing the government of Peru is far from an easy one.

BOLIVIA

Even though Bolivia has no seacoast, people traveling there from Peru often enter the country by water. Locked high in the Andes on the border between the two countries is Lake Titicaca. Lying some 12,500 feet (3,750 m) above sea level, it is the highest large lake in the world and covers as much area as does Puerto Rico, a Caribbean island that contains more than three milion people.

Though for years tourists traveled over Lake Titicaca on ocean-sized steamships, today more and more are using hydrofoils, small boats that skim rapidly over the surface of the water. Most of the people who use the lake, however, are local Indians rather than foreign tourists. And they travel either in small wooden motorboats or in traditional balsa rafts.

These balsa rafts have nothing to do with the balsa wood that comes from the coast of Ecuador. They are made entirely of reeds that have been tied into four bundles—two very fat ones that form the raft's base, and two thinner ones that form its sides. If care is taken to store the raft on dry land when not in use, it can last up to two or three years.

Most of the Indians who live around the lake speak Aymara, a language native to the Andes. They live in adobe, or mud-brick, houses clustered in close-knit communities and covering the countryside all the way from the lake to the high slopes of the Andes.

It is the ancestors of these people who probably developed the first white potato. And it is also they who invented the first freeze-

*Today's Indians still make Inca-style boats
from the tortora reeds that grow around Lake Titicaca.*

dried food. The most common form of this food is *ch'uñu.* To make it the Aymara place potatoes on an outdoor straw bed and let them freeze in the bitter cold of winter nights and melt under the bright sun of winter days. When, after a week or so, the tubers become puffy and oozy, the women of the family sluff off the slimy, outer layer with their bare feet. They then let the remaining core dry in the sun and, when it is good and dry, winnow it by sifting it in the wind on a breezy day. Potatoes dried in this fashion can be kept for years without spoiling. When the woman of the house wants to cook them, she soaks them overnight, removes any pieces of skin or eyes that remain, and steams them until they are soft. Potatoes eaten in this form are the basic staple of the Aymara.

Around Lake Titicaca, and on the immense high plateau that runs from the lake to the Argentine border and that is known as the Altiplano, the Aymara outnumber any other kind of people. But they are by no means the only group of Indians to be found there. In the southern part of this plateau most people speak Quechua, the language of the Inca. Quechua speakers dominate the population of Bolivia's valleys as well.

In both the Altiplano and the valleys, and among both Aymara and Quechua, coca chewing is a common habit. The leaf that is chewed comes from carefully tended bushes grown on the moist eastern slopes of the Andes. Harvested three to four times per year much as one would harvest tea, it is sun dried on slate patios, on cloth, or on pavement, and is then tightly packed into bundles weighing from 25 to 50 pounds (11.25 to 22.5 kg) and shipped to market. Rural people from throughout Bolivia purchase the leaf in these markets by either the ounce or pound. They chew it to give them energy when they are engaged in hard labor, to combat *soroche* (altitude sickness), and as a remedy for such common ailments as stomachaches. They also use it as an offering to the spirits, as a bribe to persuade others to come work with them, and as a gift to thank others for some favor or service.

Highland Peru has large rural populations that use coca in exactly the same way. Coca chewers in both countries are worried today that their right to use the leaf may be threatened by the way cocaine—only one of fourteen major components of the leaf—is being misused in countries like the United States. Because of illegal traffic in cocaine, there are great pressures to put an end to all coca growing. Coca chewers think that this is unfair. They argue that they use the leaf the way it was meant to be used, and that they should not have to suffer because of the misuse by people in other countries.

Ever since independence was won in 1825, the official capital of Bolivia has been Sucre, a small city far to the south of Lake Titicaca. The only part of the government that has stayed there, however, is the Supreme Court. As the result of a civil war at the end of the last century, all other government offices were moved to La Paz, the country's largest city.

The journey from Lake Titicaca to La Paz is a short one. Traveling southeast from Lake Titicaca, one comes first to the little town of Tiahuanacu, site of a great culture that flourished some two thousand years ago, where one can admire massive stone walls, intricately carved monoliths, and a large gateway carved out of a single stone block and known as the Door of the Sun. From there the road climbs over a ridge of hills, and then sweeps over a gradually rising plain until the industrial suburbs of La Paz itself come into view. Just beyond these suburbs, known as El Alto, or "the high place," the ground drops away and Bolivia's largest city lies below.

Living in La Paz is almost like living in the Grand Canyon. Because its streets climb the canyon walls, there is a difference of 3,000 feet (900 m) between one part of the city and another. The airport and the industrial suburbs lie at more than 13,000 feet (3,900 m) above sea level, the center of the city around 12,000 feet (3,600 m), and the golf course at about 10,000 feet (3,000 m). Snow may be falling in the high section near the airport at the same time that people are enjoying flowers and palm trees near the golf course.

One of the most interesting months to visit La Paz is January. In that month Indians pour into the city to celebrate one of their oldest festivals—*Alacitas.* The name of the festival comes from the Aymara word that means "buy," and the patron of the festival is the Aymara god of abundance—the *Ekeko.* Thousands of tiny fig-

ures of the *Ekeko*—loaded with all kinds of objects such as pots, pans, food, clothing, trucks, houses, money, and even coca—are sold each January. Bolivians from all levels of society buy them with the belief that if they keep an *Ekeko* near the door of their house, all the things he is carrying on his back will come their way during the year. If they already have an *Ekeko*, they may simply buy new miniatures to add to his stock.

Though the mountains, plateaus, and valleys of the Andes account for only one-third of Bolivia's territory, some two-thirds of the nation's population live there. One of the reasons for this is that practically all Aymara and Quechua speakers lived in these mountain areas when the Spaniards arrived. Another is that the mountains provide an escape from the constant heat of the lowland tropics. But perhaps the most important is the fact that the mountains contain vast stores of minerals, and the economy of Bolivia has depended heavily on mining since its beginning.

At first Bolivia's greatest wealth was the silver that came from the "rich hill" of Potosí, far south of La Paz. So much silver came from this mine during the first decades of Spanish rule that Potosí, in early colonial days, was for a time the largest city of all the Americas. Indians were forced to do most of the mining and had to climb up and down **steep shafts** with no help other than their own hands and feet. For light they often had nothing more than a candle pasted to their thumbs.

By the end of the colonial period, so much silver had been mined that Potosí went into decline. But then, about one hundred years ago, the rich deposits of tin that were lying untouched in the hill were gradually recognized as an important new source of wealth. The hill is now so honeycombed by shafts and tunnels that its top has collapsed, and there is talk of bulldozing the rest away so that all remaining minerals can be used.

Sharecropper plots reach to
the mountaintops in this view
of the Bolivian highlands.

From the mines of Bolivia comes one of the most striking dances of all South America: the *Diablada*, or "Devil's Dance." Dedicated to the spirit protector of miners—the virgin of the pits—the *Diablada* symbolizes the struggle between good and evil. In the dance, Lucifer, the prince of devils, is dressed as a fallen angel, with jewel-studded vest and skirt, velvet cape, and long, stringy hair. He is accompanied by a large group of lesser devils, some of whom act out the Seven Deadly Sins. Against these devils stands the hero of the dance, the Archangel Michael, outfitted with a light-colored skirt, shiny helmet, sparkling sword, and angel wings. During much of the dance, the Archangel loses to the devils, but in the end he is victorious, lifts his holy sword, and drives the devils back to their kingdom.

As the importance of mining declines in Bolivia, the importance of Bolivia's tropical lowlands grows. Such large deposits of natural gas have been found in the southeastern part of the country that much of it is now exported to Argentina. Sugarcane, cotton, and cattle are producing huge new fortunes. Thirty years ago, Santa Cruz—the principal city of Bolivia's lowlands—was nothing more than a tiny, isolated, and sleepy town. Today it is second in size only to La Paz and is taking an ever more important role in national politics. If this trend continues, by the end of the century, the power of the country will lie more in the lowland tropics than in the high Andes, and Bolivia will be, in effect, a different nation.

Paraguay

araguay seems to be one of the forgotten countries of the world today, hard to reach by road, plane, or ship. But this was not always so. In the early days of Spanish settlement, Paraguay was more important than Argentina, and Buenos Aires was ruled from Asunción, Paraguay's capital.

In those days the Spanish explorers thought of Paraguay as a paradise. The land was fertile. Rainfall was abundant. There were soft, rolling hills, rivers filled with fish, and forests rich in fine woods. The Indians who lived there, the Guaraní, were handsome people, simple and kind.

Paraguay has not become the paradise it promised to be, mainly because of the cruelty and greed of some of its settlers. Among the first Spaniards to come were Jesuit priests. They set up missions and began to teach the Guaraní the ways of European civilization. Soon the missions became so prosperous that other new settlers in Paraguay became jealous; they made the Jesuits leave the country and forced the Indians to work almost like slaves. Paraguay's early well-being was destroyed.

The ruins of these early missions still stand in the middle of the Paraguayan forests. Some of the buildings were beautifully constructed. Even today, though covered with trees, bushes and vines, they remain works of art—reminders of what Paraguay might have been.

There have been other tragedies in Paraguay's history. One was South America's most terrible war, when Paraguay fought alone against the nations of Uruguay, Argentina, and Brazil. The war began in 1865. By the time it was over, in 1870, more than half the people of Paraguay had been killed. Of those left, there were ten times as many females as males, and of the males, most were either young boys or old men. The country was ruined.

In 1932 Paraguay fought another war. It began as a dispute with Bolivia over who owned the Chaco, a huge piece of forested land that lay between the two countries. By 1935, when the war ended, both Bolivia and Paraguay were exhausted. Paraguay had won the war, however, and most of the Chaco has been hers ever since.

Before the Chaco War the country of Paraguay lay entirely east of the Paraguay River, and even today most of the people live in the eastern part of their country. Here the most fertile land is to be found, and Asunción, the country's capital, has been built here. The Chaco, to the west of the river, is still largely an empty territory.

Most of Paraguay's people still claim Guaraní ancestry and even speak Guaraní. In recognition of this fact, Guaraní has been declared the country's national language, even though Spanish is its official language. Since 1870, however, several small groups of Europeans have made Paraguay their home. Some of them are of Italian descent, some French, some Spanish, some English, some German, and some Swiss. Each has given its special flavor to the country and provided much-needed leadership.

Today most people who speak Guaraní have both Guaraní and Spanish ancestry and thus could be classed as *mestizo*. They are a kind and gentle people whose music, often played on the harp, is sweet sounding and unique in South America. It is this *mestizo* population that does most of the farm work of the country, even though many of them have no land of their own. In order to survive, they must often live in some deserted part of a great estate where they will raise a few crops, stay a year or two, and then move on. Many times their homes consist of only a pair of half walls and a thatched roof.

Mestizos also dominate the populations of Paraguay's towns and cities. One of these towns, Itaguá, is world famous for the beautiful lace made by its women. This lace, called *ñandutí*, is woven from very fine cotton thread and looks for all the world like finely spun spider webs.

Although most descendants of recent European migrants are prosperous and influential, and many control important businesses, some continue to work the land. East of Asunción is a colony of Swiss dairymen, whose lush farms are the pride of the nation. And west, in the midst of the great Chaco, live colonies of Mennonites.

Most of these Mennonites are descendants of pious German farmers. These Germans did not believe in war. About two centuries ago, when Germany insisted that they take up arms, they refused, left their homeland, and settled in Russia. There they lived peacefully and well for generations. But finally Russia, too, tried to make them take up arms, and they fled to Canada. When the same thing happened in that country, they turned to Paraguay and were given the promise that if they would settle the Chaco, they never again would be asked to fight.

A visit to one of these Mennonite colonies is a wonderful experience. Many of them love music. At night they bring out their favorite records, and in one of the wildest and most deserted parts of the earth, the music of Bach, Brahms, Chopin, and Schubert drifts up through the trees and into the clean, dark sky.

The Chaco, where the Mennonites live, contains a tree that has been important in Paraguay for a long time. It is called the *quebracho*, from the two Spanish words *quiebra*, or "break," and *hacha*, or "ax." The *quebracho*, then, is the "break the ax" tree, because its wood is so hard. From it comes tannin, an important product for curing leather.

In the eastern part of Paraguay grows another unusual tree, the *mate*. Its leaves are picked and ground to make a tea that millions of South Americans drink every day. Most people prepare it by putting ground *maté* leaves into a specially decorated gourd and then pouring boiling water into it. After the *maté* has steeped, they drink the mixture through a silver straw placed in the gourd.

Paraguay is one of the poorest countries of South America. Yet it still has the rich lands and pleasant climate that made it look like a paradise to the Spanish settlers. There are signs that soon this promise will be fulfilled. A new city, Ciudad Stroessner, has been built on the Brazilian border, a magnificent new bridge now spans the border, and the largest hydroelectric plant in the world is being built over the Paraná River, slated to provide so much power that Paraguay will sell vast quantities to its giant eastern neighbor. Brazilians, realizing the potential of such developments, have begun to flood into Paraguay, some as investors and others as settlers. It has been a long time in coming, but it looks as if that early dream of paradise may finally come true.

Guyana, Surinam, and French Guiana

At the northeast corner of South America lie Guyana, Surinam, and French Guiana. Until recently, the three areas were lumped together in most people's thinking and were known simply as the Guianas. They have much in common. All three have rich lowlands along the coast where most of their population live. In all three, these lowlands make up only a small part of the total territory. And in all three, most of the land is made up of plateaus and mountains known as the Guiana Highlands and is covered either with dense forests or grassy savannas.

During the early days of settlement, neither Spain nor Portugal had much interest in the Guianas. If the region contained gold or precious gems, trees hid these from sight. The climate was hot and humid, and there were no large groups of friendly Indians who could be used as servants and workers. The Guianas hardly seemed worth bothering about.

Because of this lack of interest on the part of Spain and Portugal, the Guianas eventually were split up among three northern European powers: Great Britain, the Netherlands, and France. Yet few Europeans ever wished to settle there. Immigrants were brought from other parts of the world, but always in relatively small numbers. Even today the combined populations of Guyana, Surinam, and French Guiana are less than that of Lima, Peru— and Lima is far from being the largest city of South America.

GUYANA

Guyana, a country about the size of Idaho, became fully independent only in 1970. Its movement toward independence had been a gradual one. In 1952 it had won internal self-government from Great Britain and in 1966 had become an independent member of the British Commonwealth.

The name of the country comes from a local Indian term meaning "land of waters." It was well chosen. In spite of Guyana's small size, the country has more than 600 miles (960 km) of navigable rivers and the highest waterfall in the world. Kaieteur Falls, on the Potaro River, is almost five times as high as the famous falls of Niagara.

Most of Guyana's cultivated coast lies lower than sea level and is protected by a massive series of dikes, the first of which were built by early settlers from Holland. When these settlers discovered how profitable sugarcane could be, they looked for good land where they could grow such a crop. The best, they concluded, was covered by the sea, for along great stretches of shoreline rich silt from the Amazon River had been deposited for centuries.

Most people would have thought that silt covered by sea water could not be used. But the Dutch knew, from their experience in Holland, that dikes could be built and that practically any land covered by shallow coastal waters could be reclaimed. So successful were they in reclaiming the submerged shorelands of Guyana that sugarcane remains a major product of the country to this day. Most of the people of the country live on or near such reclaimed land.

Kaieteur Falls, the highest waterfall in the world

In 1796, when French troops were occupying the Netherlands, Great Britain saw its opportunity to establish a colony in South America, and seized the Dutch colonies of the Guianas. As soon as the Dutch regained their freedom, they protested, but the matter was not settled until 1814, when French Guiana was returned to France, the Dutch regained what today is Surinam, and the British were given permanent control over the land today known as Guyana.

The people of modern day Guyana come from almost every race in the world. When the early white settlers found that there were very few native Indians who could be made to work, they began to import black slaves from Africa. But by the 1830s, the industrial revolution had reached Great Britain, and the products of the colonies had become less important. As a result, in 1834, Great Britain freed the slaves in all of her colonies. It took several years for this act of emancipation to have its full effect on the people of Guyana, but when it did, the former slaves left the plantations in droves, and the plantation owners saw that they would have to bring workers from some other part of the world if they were to survive. The continent to which they turned was Asia. As a result, today there are parts of Guyana where a traveler may think he is in India. Almost everyone is of East Indian descent. Rice is cultivated in moist paddies as it is in the Orient, and villages have Hindu temples.

Indentured labor was also brought from China. The descendants of these laborers have been joined by others who came for trade, and today the Chinese form one of the closest-knit communities of the country.

Just as some parts of Guyana seem Asian, others seem African. When the black slaves left the plantations, many of them settled in the country's great forests. There they reestablished the kind of life their ancestors had known in Africa.

In still other parts of the forest, small groups of South American Indians live. They continue to cut and burn small clearings, where they raise crops in the same way tropical forest peoples did before the white man ever discovered America.

The foods of Guyana reflect this great ethnic variety. The British brought their roast beef and meat pies, the Chinese their vegetables and noodles, the East Indians their curry, the Africans their edible roots and tubers, and the Amerindians their always-simmering pepper pot.

Except for the Bush Negro and scattered Indians, few people live in the forests of Guyana even today. Yet from this part of the country comes one of the most important products: fine tropical wood. One of the problems the people of Guyana face in shipping this wood is its weight. The best, known as greenheart, is so heavy that a log sinks in water and so hard that it breaks metal tools. Because of its density, it lasts and lasts, even when used for underwater pilings. Since it will not float, to get it to the coast, it has to be carried downstream on special pontoons.

Other riches that come from Guyana are bauxite, gold, diamonds, and manganese. Bauxite, the mineral used to manufacture aluminum, provides the country with about one-third of its income. It is so important that, in 1975, the government of Guyana nationalized the local holdings of the great North American aluminum company, Reynolds Metals. Though unpopular in the United States, the move was praised in Guyana. It stood as a symbol that, though Guyanans live in a new and small country, they have every intention of standing up for their rights.

SURINAM

Sandwiched between Guyana and French Guiana lies Surinam, formerly Dutch Guiana. It is the newest nation in South America. Although it was raised to equality with the homeland as early as 1954, only in 1975 did it become an independent republic. Surinam's population is growing very fast, but is still less than half a million.

Early white settlers in Surinam faced problems and opportunities much like those of Guyana. Here, too, currents from the great Amazon brought tons of silt to the offshore waters. And here, too, when in the nineteenth century the slaves were set free, the planters brought new workers from Asia. Although many of these came from India, just as they had in Guyana, far more came from the Dutch East Indies, and especially from Java. Whereas the Indians tended to be Hindu, the Dutch East Indians were Muslim. As a result, today Surinam has the largest population of Muslims in the Americas.

During the early history of Surinam, so many workers had been brought from Africa that, by 1790, there were fourteen black slaves for every white adult. It was with these slaves that the planters drained the shallow, offshore waters to reveal the rich silt that lay beneath. Slaves built the dikes, seawalls, and drainage ditches, and manned the sluice gates. Yet many were treated so poorly that, whenever they had a chance, they escaped into the vast jungle of the interior. There they set up villages and started a life of their own and came eventually to be known as Bush Negroes.

Today there are six recognized tribes of Bush Negroes in the Guianas—five in Surinam and one in French Guiana. Each tribe is governed by a chief or headman, and each village by a captain and a council. Bush Negro villages are known for their cleanliness and for the beauty of their woodcarving.

The largest tribe of the Bush Negroes of Surinam is the Djuka. Some of the things they do in their ritual are truly amazing. Men dance barefoot over fire, rub burning logs and sticks over their bodies, put red hot stones on their tongues, and chew jagged glass, yet never get burned or cut. No one has ever been able to explain exactly why this is so.

If bauxite is important to the economy of Guyana, it is even more important to the economy of Surinam. Only Jamaica produces more of this important metal. Agriculture, however, employs more of Surinam's workers than does bauxite mining. The principal crop is rice. Lagging far behind, but still important, are citrus fruit, coffee, and bananas. Sugar, once the major crop of the country, is grown today mainly for local consumption.

As in Guyana, the forests of Surinam contain a great deal of valuable timber. Also, as in Guyana, one of the greatest problems is getting the timber downstream and out to market.

Although the total population of Surinam is considerably smaller than that of Guyana, its capital city, Paramaribo, is much larger than Guyana's capital, Georgetown. Almost all of the older buildings in the city are made from wood so hard that, unless destroyed by fire, they will last for centuries. The streets of the city are broad and lined with beautiful trees such as royal palms, flame trees, and mahoganies. And the foods of the city are as varied as are the ancestors of its residents.

Surinam's history has not always been easy. Though it started out as a plantation society, it ran into so many problems that the number of plantations fell from eight hundred in 1790 to only ten 160 years later. Today its people have independence and have begun to realize how rich their country really is. Surinam can offer the world hydroelectric power, miles of navigable rivers, excellent schools, good government, and abundant raw materials. Understandably, its people are convinced that the future will be better than the past.

FRENCH GUIANA

French Guiana is an overseas department of the French government and sends one senator and one deputy to the National Assembly in Paris. The country is much smaller and much poorer than either Surinam or Guyana. Its total population is less than one hundred thousand.

Just as in Surinam and Guyana, most people in French Guiana live on a small part of their land—along the coast. And, as in the two neighboring countries, small groups of Bush Negroes and primitive Indians live in the jungle-filled highlands.

Most people have heard of French Guiana because of three offshore islands that were used for years as prisons. The best known was the one used for political prisoners—*Île de Diable*, or Devil's Island. Though conditions there were superior to those on the other two prison islands, *Île de Diable* was believed by many to be the worst prison in the world. So many Frenchmen became upset over its reputation that, beginning in 1938, the three island prisons were gradually closed down. The last of the convicts was shipped home in 1951.

There is great determination today to improve the image of French Guiana. To help do so, France chose the country as its principal site for the exploration of space. In its *Centre Spatial Guya-*

nais (''Guianese Space Center''), French Guiana now has the most modern equipment and plays host to the most sophisticated scientists.

Kourou, the town where the space center is located, was, until a few years ago, only a tiny, poverty-stricken village. Today it is filled with block after block of shiny new housing, lovely gardens, beachside tourist hotels, and the ultramodern buildings of the space center itself.

Cayenne, capital of French Guiana, is older than the oldest English settlement in the United States—Jamestown, Virginia. Its many ancient wooden buildings constantly remind the visitor of this fact. But it also has the sort of modern, reinforced concrete buildings that can be seen all through the Caribbean housing offices, apartments, supermarkets, and specialty shops. Just as in Paris, Cayenne has many sidewalk cafés.

The industry of French Guiana tends to be clustered around Cayenne. Two of the problems this industry faces are that wages are high and the market is small. Because so few people live in French Guiana, there is always a scarcity of labor. So attractive is the pay in the country's few urban centers that some villages in the interior of the country have been practically deserted.

The basic exports of French Guiana are wood, products made from wood, rosewood oil, shrimp, and rum. Today far more goods are brought into the country than are exported. For French Guiana to progress, this has to change. The space center has helped but cannot alone solve the problem. And so the leaders of French Guiana are looking to other possible sources of wealth, such as bauxite mining and the development of tourism. They cannot help but believe that, in spite of being a very old settlement, French Guiana has only begun to find its way.

The Giant of the South

Brazil

When the Portuguese arrived on the east coast of South America—at what is now Brazil—they found a rich and beautiful land inhabited by Indians belonging to a number of different tribes. Most of these Indians knew how to plant and harvest crops. Their tribal villages contained enormous thatched houses, so large that a single one could shelter numerous families and an entire village would contain only three or four such structures.

Each village lived unto itself and fought against all neighboring villages. Wars never seemed to end. When prisoners were taken, they were often treated like brothers and were given food, a corner in the big house, and perhaps a wife. But sooner or later they would end up as a sacrifice. Their bodies would be cut up, and the people of the village would eat the meat in an elaborate ceremony.

The Portuguese were shocked when they discovered this practice. And they were surprised when some of these people, whom they considered to be savages, asked for protection. Apparently those asking for protection were afraid that they themselves might be captured and eaten by their enemies.

The Indians taught the Portuguese many useful things. They showed them, first of all, what kinds of crops would grow in this part of the world. The most important was manioc, a root crop native to the American tropics that could be poisonous when untreated but that, when properly treated, was the staple of most people's diet.

The Indians also taught the Portuguese their language. This language, Tupi, became so important in colonial Brazil that it was finally declared *lingua geral*, or "general language." So many people spoke it that, for a time, no one was sure whether Portuguese or *lingua geral* would become the official Brazilian language.

What the Portuguese gave the Indians in return for their help was not always good. As soon as the Indians began to live and work with the white men, many of them grew sick and died. Tuberculosis, smallpox, and even the common cold killed thousands of Indians because they had no immunity to these diseases, which were new to them.

With the Indian labor force weakened, the Portuguese had to bring in workers from Africa's West Coast. These Africans brought with them many ideas and customs that are still found in Brazil's music, religion, dress, and food.

The native Indians, the Portuguese, and the African Negroes were the forebears of today's Brazilian people. They were the first ingredients of what Brazilians proudly call their melting pot. Later additions to this melting pot included people from many parts of the world. Dutch, Italians, Poles, Germans, French, Swiss, Russians, Syrians, Japanese, and even North Americans have flooded into this great land, all with the hope of getting rich.

People who travel today in Brazil, the largest country in South America, can find all sorts of contrasts. Recife, a city on the Northeast Coast, has many houses and streets that look like those of old Holland because the Dutch governed this part of the country from 1630 to 1654. Blumenau and Joinvile, towns of southern Brazil, have many brick houses with outside beams, almost exactly like those of the Pomeranian Germans who settled this part of the country more than one hundred years ago. Not far from the German settlements are towns surrounded by thousands of acres of vineyards, much like those of northern Italy. This part of Brazil was settled about a century ago by Italians.

Contrasts are found even in the parts of the country settled almost entirely by the Portuguese. Rio de Janeiro has some of the most modern and beautiful buildings in the world. Yet tens of thousands of people in this city still live in wattle and daub (stick and mud) shacks, some of them jammed right up against luxury apartments.

As a nation, Brazil is flooded with contrasts. It has many different kinds of land and climate—each with its own kind of people, with their own ways of living.

THE NORTHEAST COAST

When Brazilians think of the beginnings of their country, they usually think of the Northeast Coast. Here the first great plantations were carved out of the forest. Here the first groups of slaves were brought in. Here were the first great and wealthy families of the new country.

Sugar was the reason for the Northeast Coast's importance in colonial days. Shortly after the Portuguese learned that the fertile land was just right for growing sugarcane, Europeans developed a craving for the product. As a result, the Portuguese could sell all they could produce. To do so they needed good, cheap labor. Failing to find it in the Indian populations, they began to import slaves from Africa in such large numbers that, before long, the region had far more blacks than whites. Yet it was the whites who ran the country. Even today, descendants of these old, white Northeast Coast families hold high positions in the government. They are still some of the best educated and wealthiest people of Brazil.

On the old plantations of the Northeast Coast, the plantation owners felt very close to their slaves. In celebration of a special event such as a birthday, owners often gave a slave his freedom. Ever since these early days, then, there have been many free blacks in Brazil. The white plantation owners stayed on the land, but many of the free blacks went to the cities and acquired an education. They became physicians, lawyers, and teachers, the backbone of the urban middle class.

Not all Brazilian slaves fared so well, however. Some slave owners were so cruel that the blacks either rebelled or ran away. A number of those who escaped tried to set up kingdoms in Brazil's interior. One of these they called the Republic of Palmares. In 1645 Palmares was conquered by the Portuguese, and the blacks who lived there were either killed or sold back into slavery.

Another kingdom of ex-slaves was called Carlotta. For many years the people of Carlotta kept fine farms and mined gold. They were never conquered. It was not until the eighteenth century that they finally began to mix with the Brazilians who moved in and around their little kingdom.

Today the Northeast Coast is no longer the most important center for Brazil; the biggest cities of the country are farther south. And today plantation owners do not feel as close to their workers as they formerly did. The slaves were finally freed in 1888, and modern machinery has taken the place of the old-time *engenhos*, or hand-operated sugar mills.

For several hundred years Salvador (formerly Bahia) and Recife have been the most important cities of northeastern Brazil. They lie in the very center of the richest sugar plantations. The smaller of these two cities is Salvador, even today one of the most interesting places in South America. It is built on such a steep hill that it has been divided into two distinct parts. A giant elevator takes people from one section to the other. Most of the people of this divided city are descendants of slaves, and some of them still worship old African gods in large houses that they use as temples.

The religion practiced in these houses is known as *Candomblé*. Rather than being something straight out of Africa, it is a mixture of African beliefs, Christian beliefs, and beliefs of the native Brazilian Indians. In the states of Pernambuco and Alagoas the religion is known as *Xangô (Shangô)*, the name of an African god of thunder and lightning. In other states of the Northeast where the Indian influence is heavier, it is called *Catimbó* and emphasizes the importance of the spirits of the forest. In Rio de Janeiro and São Paulo, where it is called *Macumba*, the religion includes more Catholic elements and attracts large numbers of the middle and professional classes.

Along with their religion, the dances and songs of the blacks of the Northeast Coast have had great influence on all of Brazil. The basic rhythms of Brazilian music are rhythms that the Portuguese learned from the African slaves. And the dances are based largely on steps that were first developed for African religious ceremonies.

THE SERTÃO

Just inland from the Northeast Coast of Brazil is one of the most unusual parts of South America: the *sertão*. Here are some of the oldest towns in Brazil. Former dwellers of the *sertão* live all over the country, but today the *sertão* itself is poor and almost deserted.

Its trouble is climate. Some years, the land receives a great deal of rain. Crops such as cotton grow wonderfully. The hills blossom with a great variety of plants, and the cattle grow fat.

But most years in the *sertão* are not good. Often the rains come at the wrong time, or they do not come at all. Sometimes droughts last for years. Then the crops dry up, the hills shimmer under a blazing sun, the cattle wither away—and people leave the land and flood into other parts of Brazil.

Because life in the *sertão* is so hard, the people who still live there are always hoping for something better. First of all, they hope that droughts will not come, but they are eventually disappointed. Then they look for other kinds of escape. They begin to follow prophets who promise them a heaven on earth.

Such promises are not new in Brazil. Even before the Portuguese arrived, the Indians of the country had many legends about a grandfather thunder god. They believed that if they could reach the land where he lived, they would never have to work again. Their arrows would kill animals without anyone holding the bow. And their digging sticks would till the land without anyone picking them up. In many Indian villages, people stopped all work and danced day and night in the hope of reaching this golden land.

The prophets of the *sertão* have promised the same sort of paradise the Indians dreamed about. The most famous of the *sertão* prophets was Antonio Maciel. The people respected him so much they called him the Counselor. With him as their leader, they formed an independent state, known as the State of Good Jesus.

Because the Brazilian government was afraid of what the people of the State of Good Jesus might do, they sent armies against the Counselor and his followers. The followers, faithful to their leader, fought for almost three years against the armies, and held out until every last man and boy was dead. It finally took six thousand soldiers to defeat them.

Because they have lived in such a harsh place, the people of the *sertão* are tough. Many of the men are cowboys, for ranches cover most of the land. The *sertão* cowboys dress in tight-fitting leather trousers and high-necked leather jackets. They wear large, floppy leather hats. This kind of clothing protects them from the many thorny plants that grow in the region—and seems to say, "Look how tough we are. We belong to the *sertão* of Brazil."

THE AMAZON VALLEY

Most people think of the Amazon Valley of northern Brazil as the wildest and hottest part of South America. It is neither as wild nor as hot as they imagine. It has been explored and, in places, settled for more than three hundred years, and the temperatures are not as high as those of summer in the Mississippi Valley.

Two great cities lie in this part of Brazil. The larger one is Belém, at the mouth of the Amazon. It is full of big, beautiful homes, tree-lined boulevards, and well-kept plazas. It has a large concert hall, ultramodern office buildings, and a fine airport.

A large part of Belém was built when Brazil was still a Portuguese colony, however, and some of the most interesting sights are found in the old section of the city. Here many of the houses are covered with bright, shining, brilliantly colored tile. Some of the houses are not far from the old docks, where the many fishermen who bring in the catches from the Amazon and Para rivers tie up their boats.

The other great city of the Amazon Valley is Manaus, which lies 1,000 miles (1,600 km) up the Amazon River on a branch called Rio Negro. Some of its buildings are among the most beautiful in all Brazil. One of the largest is a glittering hotel built by a hotel owner from the United States. Here a person can enjoy a vacation in the middle of the jungle in the greatest comfort and luxury.

—56—

An even more famous building of Manaus is its opera house, built at the turn of the century. At that time, many Brazilians were making fortunes from rubber, which grew wild in the Amazon basin. They loved music and art, and they tried to make their opera house the most beautiful in all South America. Today its great dome, decorated with orange tiles set in a diamond pattern on brilliant green, still stands out above the city.

In the great days of the rubber boom, the rich people of the Amazon Valley lived almost like kings. But in 1876 an Englishman named Henry Wickham took rubber seeds to England, where they were grown. Later, plants were sent to Ceylon. From them came the enormous cultivated rubber plantations of Malaya and Sumatra. They put Brazilian wild rubber out of business.

Today most of the people of the Brazilian Amazon live in little towns strung along the edges of the rivers. There they fish, grow a little food, catch snakes and crocodiles for the skins, pick Brazil nuts, and harvest a little rubber. These towns are poor, and the inhabitants live in hope of better days.

The rivers have long been the highways for this part of Brazil. There are houses and towns on the shores of almost all the waterways, and the real tropical forest exists only at a distance from the rivers. Only there can a person find the primitive Indians who have made the region famous.

The Amazon Valley covers almost half of Brazil, as well as parts of Venezuela, Colombia, Ecuador, Peru, and Bolivia. The river drains almost half of all South America. At its mouth it is so big that it holds an island larger than the country of Belgium. Two hundred miles (320 km) out to sea the ocean water is still muddy from the topsoil it carries along, topsoil that has been converted into rich agricultural land along the coasts of the Guianas.

Away from the edges of the Amazon and its branches, the immense river valleys are nearly empty. But change is coming quickly. One road already cuts through 1,000 miles (1,600 km) of the Amazon jungle and connects Belém with Brasília, the country's capital. Another road links Brasília with Acre, far to the west. Still other roads are being pushed along the north and south banks of the Amazon itself.

As soon as these roads open, rich and poor alike pour into the

Amazon basin. From the poverty-stricken, arid lands of the *sertão*, simple farmers come, settle in new farming clusters called *agrovilas*, and try to make the land produce. And along some of the richest floodplains, Japanese farmers have built their homes and have begun to grow black pepper and jute.

Not all attempts to develop the Amazon have worked, however. In 1967 an American by the name of Daniel K. Ludwig bought a 5,600-square-mile (14,560-sq-km) tract for seventy-five cents an acre (.4 ha). Having great visions of what could be done, he poured $559 million of his own money and $304 million in borrowed funds into starting tree farms, thinking that the climate of the Amazon would be ideal for the production of paper pulp. To this end, he imported an entire floating pulp factory from Japan, built towns for his workers, and developed a mine to produce kaolin, a fine white powder used to coat magazine paper. But the trees that were planted were not well suited to the poor soils of that part of the Amazon, and so grew slowly and were scrawny and scraggly. Because the trees did not produce well, the huge pulp mill was idle most of the time, and problems with workers were constant. Despite much effort and dedication, for fifteen long years Ludwig lost money. By that time he was eighty-four years old. Tired and discouraged, he sold out to a group of twenty-two Brazilian companies that had the support of the Brazilian government's Bank of Brazil.

In spite of such experiences, many Amazonian treasures still remain to be found. Great deposits of iron and bauxite have already been located. There may be many other metals hidden beneath the trees. Today man seems to be learning how to live in the Amazon and how to use its resources. As he learns more, the Amazon is bound to become one of the most important parts of the world.

THE CENTRAL EAST

The real heart of Brazilian life today lies more than 1,500 miles (2,400 km) south of the Amazon, in the Central East. Here are fine ports, fertile soil, and rich mines.

When the Portuguese first came to Brazil, they thought the

Central East was one of the poorest parts of the land. They changed their minds, however, when gold was discovered there in 1698. Between 1700 and 1800 almost half of all the gold mined in the world came from east-central Brazil. Tiny towns lost in the mountains grew wealthy overnight. The richest of these, Ouro Preto, became a center for art and culture. Its churches and homes were filled with beautiful carvings and paintings. One of its artists, named Aleijandinho, has often been called the best sculptor South America has ever had. So dedicated was he to his work that when his hands became terribly deformed with leprosy, he had his assistant tie his tools to the stumps of his fingers so that he could continue to shape the stone.

Because Aleijandinho's work is so beautiful and because Ouro Preto is so full of other art treasures, the Brazilian government made the city a national monument in 1933. Today fourteen thousand people reside in the living museum. They are surrounded by the empty shells of buildings that once housed more than sixty thousand residents.

Even though it is small, Ouro Preto has been important in Brazilian history. Its gold made fabulous Rio de Janeiro grow. In 1700 Rio was nothing more than a tiny defense post. Then the people of Ouro Preto began to use it as a port. Almost overnight the defense post grew into a boom town. By 1762 it had become so large and important that the government of colonial Brazil decided to move there from the old center of Bahia.

The growing importance of Rio did not stop there, however. In 1807 Napoleon invaded Portugal, and the Portuguese king fled to Brazil. Once there, he made Rio de Janeiro the capital of the entire Portuguese empire. Fourteen years later, his son Pedro separated Brazil from Portugal. On December 1, 1822, he was crowned Pedro I, Emperor of Brazil. Emperors ruled Brazil until 1889.

It is only in the past eighty years, however, that Rio has become the great modern center that people know today. Many travelers consider it the most beautiful city in the world. It has fine modern buildings and is surrounded by striking mountains and shimmering white beaches. Great boulevards run between the shore and the mountains, and formal gardens stretch for miles.

*Mountains provide a dramatic background
for the Rio de Janeiro skyline
as it is seen from Ipanema beach.*

Rio has been the center of Brazilian life for almost two hundred years. Yet in 1960 the government moved its offices to Brasília, a new city far in the interior of the country. Today Rio is no longer the capital of the greatest nation in South America.

The Central East of Brazil contains many other cities, some of them quite important. One of them, Belo Horizonte, was founded in 1897 to take the place of the old town of Ouro Preto. Before Brazilians built Belo Horizonte, they planned it completely. As in Washington, D.C., all its streets and boulevards were laid out before any houses were started.

Another important city of the Central East is Volta Redonda. Here the Brazilians have built the largest steel plant in South America. Much of the steel that comes from its blast furnaces has gone into new buildings in the fastest-growing center of all east-central Brazil, São Paulo.

Like many other Brazilian cities, São Paulo is very old; a mission was founded there in 1554. Yet as late as 1883 the city had only thirty-five thousand inhabitants. Then suddenly it began to grow, because of coffee.

Toward the end of the last century, when Paulistas (the people of São Paulo) learned that the land around their city was perfect for growing coffee trees, they began to bring millions of workers from Europe. Because of these European workers, São Paulo's land, and the world's taste for coffee, many of the city's people have become tremendously wealthy. São Paulo has become one of the most active business centers in South America. All around it, giant coffee *fazendas*, or estates, cover the land, with long, straight rows of coffee trees running over the hillsides.

The coffee harvest begins in May and lasts until August. The workers pick the coffee beans and carry them to the center of the *fazenda*. There they are dumped into large tanks of water, where the green beans and the sticks and stones are separated from the ripe beans. Then the ripe beans are carried to huge drying platforms made of black tile. On these, the beans are raked over and over again. If it rains, they are quickly gathered up and covered with canvas. Finally, when they are dry through and through, they are put into machines that husk them and separate them by weight, size, and shape. Only then do they go into the bags that are sent to all parts of the world, where the coffee beans are roasted and blended and ground into the coffee we know.

Today coffee is not so important as it used to be in east-central Brazil. São Paulo has become the major industrial center for all Brazil, manufacturing everything from combs to automobiles. The Paulistas brag about this prosperity to anyone who will listen. They know that, on the South American continent, theirs is the most important city of commerce.

THE SOUTH

Of all parts of the country, the South is the least Brazilian. Here the land has been settled mostly by people from Europe. Until World War II, large numbers of these people taught their children in the languages of their native lands. Then the Brazilian government ruled that all children born in Brazil had to be educated in Portuguese.

Most of the Brazilians of recent European extraction live on small farms. If their ancestors were German, they might raise rye, potatoes, and hogs. If their ancestors were Italian, they might raise grapes.

But not all the land of the South has been turned over to the newcomers. Some of it is made up of great *pampas*, or plains, where cattle are raised. Here the cowboys, or *gauchos*, are descended from early white settlers and Indian women. Their costume is unusual. They often wear *bombachas*, or baggy bloomer pants. Around their necks they tie large bandannas, and on their heads they wear flat-topped hats with the brims turned up.

The *gauchos* spend a great part of their lives on their horses. So close do they feel to these animals that they have a saying, "A man without his horse is like a man without his pants." They produce one of the favorite foods of the poor people of Brazil: *carne seca*, or dried beef. Every year great stacks of this preserved meat are shipped to all parts of the country.

Other parts of the South have rice *fazendas*, whose owners and workers usually come from Brazilian or Portuguese families.

As in so many other parts of the country, the estates are huge and the estate owners live in luxury. But many of the workers are very poor.

When coffee brought so much prosperity to the state of São Paulo, people living in southern Brazil thought that it could bring prosperity to them as well. In the state of Paraná, hundreds of thousands of acres of coffee trees were planted, only to be killed by frost when they were a few years old. The lesson was a hard one, but the people finally had to admit that, though they lived in Brazil, they hardly lived in the tropics.

The cities of southern Brazil are some of the fastest growing in the entire country. The largest is Porto Alegre, which today has about one million people. After São Paulo, Rio, and Belo Horizonte, it is the most important business center in Brazil. It takes hides from the *gauchos* and tans them into leather. It takes wool from the sheep herders of the *pampas* and turns it into yarn and clothing. It takes grapes from the Italians and turns them into wine. And it takes hops from the Germans and turns them into beer.

THE CENTRAL WEST

Until a very few years ago, the Central West was, for the Brazilians, the "wild West." As late as 1940, a person always carried a gun in this part of the country. Most of the land was used as open range. Cattle roamed over the countryside with hardly a fence in sight.

Today the Central West has become a new and different land. Brazilians have "moved to the frontier."

The idea that the people of Brazil should move away from the seacoast is an old one. As long ago as colonial days there was talk of shifting the capital into the interior. In every Brazilian constitution since 1889 there has been a section ordering the building of a new capital city. Finally, in 1957, the Brazilian congress decided it was time to carry out this order.

The congress chose a site about 1,000 miles (1,600 km) from the sea, in high country, 3,900 feet (1,170 m) above sea level. Here would be a pleasant climate, with an average temperature of about 68°F (20°C). The name of the city was to be Brasília. April 21, 1960, was set as the date when the government would move from Rio de Janeiro; Brasília, as a city, was to be finished in 1961.

When the Brazilian congress announced its decision, many people thought it was just an impossible dream. How could the Brazilians build a complete city in only three years?

But Juscelino Kubitschek, the president of the country, was determined. He ordered sixty thousand workers to be hired. It took only thirty-three months for the city to be readied to welcome the government. Just as the congress had planned, the president moved in on April 21, 1960.

Every person, no matter where he lives, should be proud that men could build such a beautiful place as Brasília in so short a time. The city is shaped like an airplane. The body of the plane contains the houses of congress, the courts, and the ministries. The wings of the plane contain long rectangular blocks of apartments. Starting at the head of the plane body and reaching back around the wing tips is a giant artificial lake, on the shores of which stands the presidential palace.

The city planner and the architect for the buildings were chosen through an open competition. Since the top two won, the city has turned out to be a living museum of modern design. But even the best of intentions could not avoid certain problems. Many of the government workers, used to living in beautiful Rio de Janeiro, disliked the flat scenery, the isolation, and the lack of cultural activities in the new city. As a result, they either gave up their jobs or, for years, commuted regularly between Rio and Brasília, looking on the new capital as an interesting place to visit but not to live. The designers had planned for stores to look inward to parks and patios, so that people could enter and leave by foot, without having to face heavy traffic. But store owners were so accustomed to facing

This sculpture in Brasília is in keeping with the modern design of the capital city, which was constructed in thirty-three months.

busy streets that many began to use their delivery, or back, doors as main entrances. Finally, the workers who built Brasília, many of whom had come out of the poverty-stricken *sertão*, found that once the city was completed, they wanted to stay there. But they could not afford the high prices and rents they would have to pay to live in one of the beautiful new high-rise buildings. Consequently, they continued to live in the shanties that they had thrown up on the edge of town as temporary housing. Today these shanties have become permanent, and workers not only have to live in poor housing, but, to get to work, they have to travel the long distances that separate their shantytowns from the city.

Brazilians love their country deeply. When they stumble across one of its problems, they simply roll up their sleeves and get to work. One of their current problems is energy. Though Brazil has many resources, it has relatively little oil, and its coal is of poor quality. To solve this particular problem, the Brazilian government created a national petroleum company, Petrobras. Through the efforts of this company, Brazil produces far more oil than it ever dreamed possible. But still it is not enough. To help take up the slack, the country has begun to produce immense quantities of gasohol, discovering that not only sugarcane but even bamboo can be used for this purpose. To insure that this new energy source will be used, it has ordered the country's automobile factories to manufacture engines that will run on gasohol. Finally, it has turned more and more to its great water resources. Because of the country's many rivers, mountains, and hills, it has been able to build some of the largest hydroelectric plants in the world.

Brazilians are proud of the fact that they have the largest country in South America, and that they account for about half of the people of that continent. They are convinced that the best is yet to come, that Brazil is destined to become one of the leaders of the world.

Farthest and Nearest

Uruguay, Argentina, and Chile

In distance, Uruguay, Argentina, and Chile are the neighbors farthest from North America, but in spirit they are nearest. Many places in these three countries look like parts of North America and Europe, and many of the people think, dress, and act almost the same as do people in North America and Europe.

URUGUAY

Next to Surinam, Uruguay is the smallest of the twelve independent nations of South America. It came into being thanks largely to the intervention of Great Britain. For years, both the Portuguese and the Spaniards had laid claim to this land, and when Brazil and Argentina became free nations, both continued to press these claims. Great Britain then stepped in, offered to settle the dispute, and suggested that Uruguay go its own separate way. In 1828 Uruguay was set up as an independent buffer state between Brazil and Argentina. The solution proved to be a happy one. Today Uruguay's relations with its two giant neighbors are very good.

After independence, Uruguay had to struggle to get on its feet. Like all South American countries, it had its share of dictators. But in 1903 one of the greatest men in South American history became president. His name was José Battle y Ordóñez. Battle (Bahje), as the Uruguayans call him, had many ideals for his country. He wanted to make it a "Switzerland of South America." In Switzerland, a federal council of seven members holds executive power; there is no strong president. Until Battle died in 1929 he fought for his ideals, and his influence was so great that some of his plans were carried out even after his death. Because of Battle, Uruguay received advanced social welfare laws and, from 1952 to 1967, was ruled by a council instead of a president. The welfare laws rivaled those of Sweden, known for its progressive social welfare system, and the council was patterned after the one that had governed Switzerland for centuries. By trying these ideas, Uruguayans shared in Battle's dream of making their country a model of democracy for all Latin America.

But Uruguay's economy was not as strong as Sweden's, nor were the Uruguayan people like the Swiss. By 1967 their country faced such severe economic problems that they had to lower some of their social welfare benefits and revert to the more decisive rule of a president.

By the time that happened, the economy had suffered so much that the country entered a period of great social unrest. Guerrilla groups formed, especially in Montevideo, Uruguay's capital. Tens of thousands of the best-trained citizens left the country, never to return. Finally, to bring some sort of order out of the chaos, the military took over the government. In a country long accustomed to freedom of speech, strict controls were imposed. Businesses went bankrupt, books were removed from libraries, the universities were closed, and certain activities and professions thought not to be supportive of the government were simply outlawed.

It has taken a long time for Uruguayans to recover from those difficult days. But that recovery has gradually come about. The government tries to interfere less in the life of the average citizen than it did before, and a new emphasis is being placed on private business. While this has not solved all the economic problems, it has helped a great deal.

The principal basis of the Uruguayan economy is livestock farming. About 80 percent of the country's total area is used for this purpose. For every man, woman, and child, Uruguay has more than three head of cattle and ten head of sheep. This makes the country, in spite of its small size, one of the most important producers of meat, hides, and wool in the world.

Uruguay is mostly a country of softly rolling grasslands broken by small, dense forests along the river bottoms. In the southern part of the country these grasslands have been plowed up, and here hundreds of thousands of descendants of recent European immigrants have planted small farms. In the center of this farming region is the one large city of the country: Montevideo, its capital. About half of all Uruguayans live there.

There are many things that Uruguayans love about their capital, but four of them stand out above the rest. These are the meat markets, the soccer stadium, the theaters, and the beaches.

Uruguayans so love meat that the average person eats more than a pound a day. Their favorite meat dish is the *aparrillada*, or "mixed grill." To prepare it they roast over hot coals an enormous variety of sausages and cuts of beef and veal. Combined with french fries, salad, and wine, it makes a banquet.

As to soccer, the stadium in Montevideo is one of the largest in the world. The Uruguayans fill it to overflowing. The country's soccer teams are excellent. They have held the world championship in the sport, defeating even such nations as Germany and England.

Uruguayans love the arts, too. Besides many theaters, there are several concert halls in Montevideo where Uruguayans can enjoy some of the finest soloists in the world, their own national symphony, and outstanding theater and ballet groups.

The beaches are fantastic. They begin near downtown Montevideo and stretch out on both sides of the city. To the east they reach the borders of Brazil. At about midpoint along that coast, the Uruguayans have built the most famous resort in all of South America: Punta del Este. Twenty years ago Punta del Este was a tranquil village of picturesque, small houses and manicured gardens. Today downtown Punta del Este looks like an extension of Montevideo itself, for it is filled with high-rise condominiums.

Since Uruguay was settled largely during the past one hundred

After defeating Brazil, the Uruguayan soccer team
and fans celebrate in the moat between the stands
and the playing field at Centenario Stadium.
The victory is like David beating Goliath.

and fifty years, many of its people take pride in tracing their ancestry back to Europe. Hence Christmas, which comes on one of the hottest days of summer, is celebrated much as it is in Europe. People set up Christmas trees in their living rooms, decorate them with artificial snow, exchange presents, and eat heavy sweet breads, candies, and nuts. But they also flood to the beaches, for one of the Christmas customs is to have a picnic alongside the ocean.

Most Uruguayans are descended from Spaniards and Italians. But the country also holds colonies of Swiss, English, and German descent.

One of the most interesting of such colonies is that established by the Waldensians, or Valdenses. These people occupy a part of the country that is larger than the state of Connecticut. They had their beginnings in Lyons, France, about 1170, and were Protestants three hundred years before the Protestant Reformation. Their leader was named Peter Valdo. When they were expelled from their own country, some of them took refuge in the mountains of northern Italy. There they stayed and fought for their beliefs for centuries.

During the past one hundred years, the promise of religious freedom has brought many Waldensians to Uruguay. In this new country they have built up fine, rich farms, and successful businesses.

Today many Waldensians still speak old-style French among themselves, but they feel completely at home in their new country. Like their fellow Uruguayans, they often say that, in spite of its problems, Uruguay is the best country in the world.

ARGENTINA

People who travel from Montevideo to Buenos Aires, the capital of Argentina, cross the second largest river in South America. Although it is known in Spanish as the "River of Silver" (*Rio de la Plata*), in English it is simply called the River Plate. It is so wide that ships crossing from Montevideo to Buenos Aires can take all night and airplanes flying between the two cities can lose sight of land.

The northern bank of this great river is lined with the beautiful white sand beaches that make Uruguay a vacation paradise. But its southern bank is covered with the vast mud flats that form the edge of the great South American *pampa*, a plain so flat that it looks like the sea itself.

On these mud flats has been built the city of Buenos Aires. So that large ships may reach its port, a deep channel has been dug. But so much mud washes down from the rich farmlands of Uruguay and Argentina that men must work constantly to keep the channel open.

Greatness came to Buenos Aires only during the past hundred years. During much of the colonial period, the city was ruled from little Asunción, in Paraguay. As late as 1855, Buenos Aires had only ninety thousand people. Then settlers from many different European nations flooded into the *pampa*, and tiny Buenos Aires became one of the great cities of the world.

The center of the city was built at a time when France's influence in South America was strong. And so the city, even today, has hundreds of buildings designed in the French manner, with balconies, turrets, towers, and mansard, or double-sloped, roofs. The sidewalks are tiled and graced in summer with open-air cafés and restaurants. Flower stalls and magazine stands brighten downtown street corners. There are even open-air bookstalls, very much like the ones found in Paris.

Among the many groups that have left their mark on the city are the British. Near the docks and facing the largest train station is a red brick bell tower donated by Great Britain. And on the main shopping street the largest department store is Harrods, a branch of the famous Harrods store of London.

Though the total number of British who settled in Argentina was never large, their influence has been important. It was the British who brought the first refrigerator ship, making it possible to export more and better meat from the *pampas*. It was they who brought in money to start many of the first factories, and it was they who managed the building of the railroads. Perhaps most important of all, it was the British who imported the first full-blooded cattle. Even today English Herefords and Scottish Aberdeen Angus are the two most respected breeds of cattle on the country's vast ranches.

Because of the importance of the British to the economy, a number of their social customs took root in Argentina as well. People who live in Buenos Aires today love tea almost as much as do the English, and some of the city's thousands of tearooms still have English names. One of the city's favorite sports is polo, an ancient game brought to England in 1869 from India, and carried from England to Argentina by young Anglo-Argentines.

One of the reasons that polo is so popular is that it is played on horseback, and Argentines, with their ranching background, love horses. To play the game, each rider takes a long-handled mallet, with which he tries to drive the one polo ball past his opponents and into the goal.

Most people who live in Buenos Aires today are descendants, not of the French or British, but of hundreds of thousands of Italians and Spaniards who immigrated to the *pampas* during the past one hundred years. But the dyed-in-the-wool Argentine comes from none of these groups. Rather he traces his ancestry to the native Indians of the *pampas*, the early Spanish settlers, or a combination of the two. Many of these native Argentines have traditionally been *gauchos*, the term used for the cowboys of southern Brazil, Uruguay, and Argentina. When they were gauchos, they may well have played a horseback game of their own called "duck" (*pato*). In its pure form this game centered around a duck placed in the middle of the playing field. Each player, while still on horseback, tried to reach down, pick it up by the neck, and then either hurl it to another member of his team or make a goal with it himself. The game is still played today, though a heavy ball covered by a series of rounded handles has been substituted for the live duck.

More than half of all Argentines live either in Buenos Aires or on the immense *pampas* surrounding it, and most of the products that Argentina exports come from this part of the country as well. Yet the *pampas* make up only a small part of the whole. In the north, a large section, the Chaco, is covered by scrub vegetation, just like the Chaco in Paraguay. And as in Paraguay, it produces *quebracho* wood.

To the west of the Chaco is a part of Argentina that produces maize and sugarcane. This was one of the first regions to be settled, the settlers moving there from the area of the central Andes. Even today the cities and the people of this part of the country look as though they belong more to Peru and Bolivia than to Argentina. The most important city of this region is Tucumán.

South of Tucumán the land gets drier. A few rivers rush down the Andes, however, and where these make oases, people have settled. They specialize in growing grapes, from which they make wine. Today Mendoza, the largest city of this wine-making region, produces some of the best wines of the world.

From the southern edge of the great *pampa* to the tip of South America stretches Patagonia, the largest and most deserted part of the country. It is cold, dry, and terribly windy. The few houses that exist tend to be located along riverbeds, or at the base of canyons, where there is a bit of water as well as protection from the constant wind.

Some of the first settlers of Patagonia were Welshmen. Others were English, Scottish, and, of course, native Argentines. By working together these groups have built enormous sheep ranches in the area, some of which are more than 100 miles (160 km) square.

Two of the tips of Patagonia are especially interesting. All along the western edge, as the land climbs up into the Andes mountains, bounteous rain falls. Here magnificent forests have taken root. Some of them look down on mirrorlike lakes. Around the most beautiful, Germans and Swiss have settled. In summer, tourists come to fish and hike, and in winter, they ski.

The towns that have been built to take care of these tourists are among the most beautiful of South America. The largest is called Bariloche. So popular has it become that its streets have begun to suffer from traffic jams, and apartment buildings have begun to block the view of its lovely lake.

The other unusual part of Patagonia is the very tip of the continent—really not a part of South America itself, but an island, Tierra del Fuego—partly in Argentina and partly in Chile. Though

Tierra del Fuego is really a very cold place, its name means "Land of Fire," because when early European explorers first saw it, Indians were burning many fires along its shores. These Indians were among the most primitive people to be found anywhere. The Yahgan, one of the tribes, lived off seals, fish, mussels, gulls, and birds' eggs. The waters were icy, and only the women knew how to swim. Their husbands rowed them out in little canoes, and the women swam off and clubbed seals or dived down and brought up the mussels. White men were surprised to see these hardy people walking around naked, even when snow was falling.

Today, almost all the Indians of Tierra del Fuego have died of white men's diseases, and there are sheep ranches all over the island. The southern shore even has a city, Ushuaia, the southernmost town in the world.

A few hundred miles to the northeast of Tierra del Fuego lies a group of islands, named the Falklands by the British, that have been the subject of international debate for two hundred years. They were first discovered in the sixteenth century, and have been claimed by at least four major nations: France, Spain, Great Britain and Argentina.

The French were the first to attempt to settle the place, though their settlement lasted only three years, from 1764 to 1767. Next came the British, whose first settlement lasted eight years, from 1766 to 1774. When the Spanish protested both settlements, claiming prior ownership on the basis of rights of discovery, the French voluntarily withdrew, and the Spanish government paid them for the investment they had made. The British, however, asked permission to remain, and were allowed to do so with the understanding that their settlement would in no way affect Spanish sovereignty over the area. Once the French departed, the Spanish established a military post on the site of the French settlement and retained it until 1810, when they had to withdraw their forces to meet challenges to Spanish authority on the South American mainland.

In 1826, basing its rights on the historic claims of the Spanish crown, the government of newly created Argentina began resettling the islands and asserting authority over fishing and sealing activities. In 1829 its garrison captured two American ships that were hunting seals without permission. In reprisal, an American warship, the *Lexington*, sailed into the islands' main harbor, destroyed the Argentine settlement, arrested the governor and his guards, and charged them with piracy. This left the Falklands abandoned once again and opened the door for British reoccupation.

The new British settlement was established in 1833. From the beginning the Argentines opposed it, but without success. Finally, in April 1982, after 150 years of fruitless protest, they decided to invade the islands and claim by force what they had never been able to obtain through international diplomacy. In justification of their act, they argued that the British had always been there illegally, and that they had never really populated the islands or developed their economy. They had a point. In the 150 years that the British had occupied the Falklands, about all that they had accomplished was to build a few small towns and raise hundreds of thousands of sheep. At the time of the Argentine invasion, the islands' population was only a little over 1,800 people.

Given the historic neglect of the islands by Great Britain, that country's swift and violent reaction came as a great surprise to the Argentines. As soon as the British government learned of the invasion, it announced its resolve to protect the rights of the Falklanders by retaking the islands, and dispatched its great fleet to accomplish that mission as rapidly as possible. Sea, air and land battles lasted some ten weeks, during which time both Argentine and British ships and planes were destroyed, and many young men from both sides lost their lives. In the end the Argentine troops, surrounded in Port Stanley, the capital of the islands, raised white flags in surrender.

Argentines were baffled by the resolution of the British and were disappointed that the United States took the British side. They had always thought that they could count on the support of all American nations against any European power.

In spite of such disappointments, the people of Argentina continue to think of themselves as the most European of all Latin

*Children pull their homemade sleds up a slope
near the camp of Goose Green, the site of some of the
bloodiest fighting in the battle of the Falklands.*

Americans and in many ways similar to the people of the United States. A fairly small group of them ran the country the way they wished until, a little more than thirty years ago, a man by the name of Juan Perón came to power. Though ranching had been the main source of wealth for the country for centuries, Perón thought that industry was needed. He also thought that the workers deserved more power than they had.

The changes Perón made brought many problems to the country. For the first time in generations, Argentina began to go backward rather than forward. Because there were so many problems, groups of guerrillas formed and began to make direct attacks on the rich. Things became so bad that finally the military decided they would have to take over.

It will take many years for Argentina to recover from the disasters of the past thirty years. Many Argentine workers think that Perón was their greatest hero. Businessmen tend to think that he was their worst enemy. Their differences of opinion have been so great that they have inspired the writing of many books and even one musical comedy. Called *Evita*, that musical comedy became one of the hits of the season when it was first presented in New York. People who saw it realized that they were not only being entertained, they were also learning an important lesson of history.

CHILE

West of Argentina, on the other side of the Andes, lies Chile, a giant, long and narrow ribbon of a country. Its coast stretches 2,900 miles (4,640 km) from the subtropics to the subarctic, yet nowhere is the country more than 221 miles (354 km) wide. In its north is desert, in its center farmland, and in its south vast forests.

The Atacama Desert of northern Chile is so dry that it has one of the few weather stations in the world where no rain has ever been recorded. At one time the valleys in this part of the country were covered with lakes. Little by little these lakes dried up, leaving behind rich deposits of minerals. For centuries people passed the desert by, thinking that it was good for nothing. Then, in 1809, a German discovered that nitrate, one of the most abundant minerals, could be used for fertilizer. Later in the century, it was discovered that nitrate could be used for explosives as well. With these discoveries, the desert suddenly became important—so important that Chile went to war against Peru and Bolivia to expand its holdings in the region.

During World War I, when trade with Chile was difficult and, at times even impossible, European scientists invented artificial nitrate. Since that time natural nitrate has become less important. Copper is now the leading product of the Chilean north.

Many of the mining towns and cities of northern Chile sit in the middle of the most absolute desert of the world. Chuquicamata, one of the largest of the copper mines, is a good example. To supply workers there, the mining company had to pipe water in from the high Andes and import all the food that was eaten.

The real heart of Chile is its great central valley. Here the Incas set up the southernmost outposts of their empire, and here the first successful Spanish settlements were established. Here also lived the largest of Chilean Indian groups: the Araucanians.

The Incas had discovered that the Araucanians were some of the fiercest and most independent of all South American Indians and were still struggling against them when the Spaniards arrived. For more than three hundred years after conquest, the Spaniards themselves continued the fight. But they never won it. Peace has reigned for less than a century, and when it came, it was through the Indians' free will; they had never been defeated.

Although the early Spaniards were disappointed because they failed to find precious metals in Chile, increasing numbers were drawn over the years by the land's rich soil and pleasant climate. The central valley reminded many Spaniards of Andalucia, a Spanish province from which many of them had come.

Since there were few white women among the early settlers, soon each Spaniard arranged to be attended by one or even several Indian women. Their descendants were neither Spanish nor Indians; they were *mestizo*, or simply Chileans. Most people in the country come from just such a background.

The town site and operations plant of El Teniente, the world's largest underground copper mine, is on this remote, 8,000-foot (2,400-m) high mountainside.

As has happened with so many other countries of South America, Chile has received immigrants from many different nations. The man who led Chile's struggle for independence was Bernardo O'Higgins. His father, born in Ireland, worked in his early years as a simple peddler but eventually became viceroy of all Peru. The son, Bernardo, not only helped free Chile, but also became one of its first chiefs of state and the first South American leader to give freedom to the slaves.

Another great leader of Chilean independence was the Englishman, Lord Cochrane. The free Chilean navy that he organized and commanded, though small, helped give the final blow to Spanish power in the continent.

As important as these descendants of the British Isles are to Chilean history, most Chileans are descended either from early Spanish settlers or Araucanian Indians and have deep roots in the land. When Chile was first colonized by the Spaniards, its richest lands were divided up among only a few favored Spanish-speaking colonists. As a result, certain old families of Spanish origin have owned great estates for generations, have stayed on the land, have traditionally felt close to their workers, and have time and again provided political, economic, and social leadership.

Most Chileans have never been so favored. Whether they are of Spanish descent, of mixed descent, or of pure Indian descent, they have had to live by the sweat of their brow. Those who served the great estates were known as *inquilinos*, or "tenants." Their life was hard, similar to that of a sharecropper in the old, Deep South. When they left in hopes of finding a better future in some city of the country, their fortune was often so tragic that they came to be know as *rotos*, or "broken ones."

The *rotos* have become the backbone of modern Chile. They work in the mines of the northern desert, man thousands of urban factories, and produce copper, nitrate, cement, glass, soap, paper, matches, shoes, sugar, steel, and all the other modern products for which Chile has come to be known. It is largely their hard work that has made Santiago into a bustling, modern city, and has made Chile itself a leader of industry. But their repeated tragedies and suffering have made many of them bitter and envious. As a result,

—81—

in the early 1970s, they banded together, demanded social justice, and supported the first duly elected socialist government in the Americas. That government, headed by President Salvador Allende, managed to stay in power only three years. It had tried to improve the lot of the *inquilinos* by declaring agrarian reform, and to improve the lot of the *rotos* by taking control of much of Chile's basic industry. But, as the changes helped the poor, they threatened the rich. So many of the rich became afraid they would lose their privileges that they were happy when the armed forces staged a revolution and even when Allende himself was killed.

With the revolution came military government, a loss of Chile's most treasured democratic traditions, and even oppression. For many decades, Chile had been admired as a civilized, open nation and a lover of freedom. But the events of the 1970s have left their mark. Even if Chile recovers its full democracy, it will be a different place, for its masses have been wakened and will not easily sleep again.

The central valley of Chile, traditional home of the great estates, the *patrones*, and the *inquilinos*, is a land of mud walls, whitewashed mud buildings with thatched or red tile roofs, roads lined with stately Lombardy poplars and drooping willows, and fields overflowing with wheat and grapes. Southern Chile seems to belong to a different world. The farther south the land lies, the more rain it receives. Just south of the Bio-Bio River, the fields are rolling, hedged with trees, and filled with grain crops. But in the deep south, below Valdivia, most of the land is covered with forest so dense and wet that it cannot be burned off. Fjords—deep, narrow bays—bite into the coast, much as they do in Norway. Rain is so constant and the land is so sodden that, even today, few people want to live there.

Until 1850 practically all the land south of the Bio-Bio River was left to the Araucanians. Then Germans began to arrive. Though their numbers were never great, they showed what could be done with the land. The farms they built and the houses they erected looked very much like the ones they had left behind in Germany. Even today their communities look as if they belong more to Europe than to the Americas.

Though the influence of these German colonists has been great in southern Chile, it is the Chilean *roto* who has really populated the region. Like their German counterparts, they are hard workers. Most of their farms are small, their houses wooden and roofed with either shingles or iron, and their fields used for cattle, grains, or timber.

Practically all of Chile suffers from earthquakes. In the south they are particularly severe. Yet they have brought great beauty to the land, fashioning mountain lakes of many different colored waters, some a deep, clear blue, some a milky green, and some a vibrant emerald. The most impressive mountain peak of the region is the volcano, Osorno. It is perfectly conical and tipped with snow, and looks very similar to the famous Mount Fujiyama of Japan.

Making a home in such a violent land is not easy. When an earthquake comes and towns and cities are destroyed, people can be forced to sleep in the streets and plazas. Sometimes the land has changed so much that new maps have had to be drawn. Yet, when such things have happened, the men and women of southern Chile have not wanted to leave. They have looked to the richness of the soil, to the beautiful lakes, fields, beechwoods, and mountains, and they have begun to rebuild.

So This Is South America

This, then, is South America, a continent of both contrasts and problems. In the past seventy years its cities have become very modern, aircraft have revolutionized its system of transport, and radio and television have come into millions of homes.

Those most benefitting from such changes live in the cities of the continent. But enormous numbers of people still live in the countryside, and there life has often gone on just as before. In many places, farmers still work their land in the same way their ancestors did three or four hundred years ago. Many country people still have no electricity or running water, and some have no access to either schools or hospitals.

There are signs, however, that things are changing. As the farmers and workers of South America learn how farmers and workers live on other continents, they are realizing that they do not have to be poor and ignorant forever. They are beginning to look for a better way of life. With great hope, millions are moving to the cities. There, in spite of that hope, most end up living in mammoth slums and facing a constant fight for daily food.

The desire of such people for a more pleasant way of life has brought many conflicts to the continent. Some South American governments have responded with sweeping land reforms and with the nationalization of major industries. Other governments have limited freedom of expression in an attempt to keep things as they are. When this has happened, worker and student groups have issued passionate calls for social justice and have even entered into armed rebellion.

South Americans want their continent for themselves. They deeply resent all foreign influence, especially that of the United States. Increasing numbers are so disappointed with their capitalist past that they are looking to socialism or communism as the only means of improvement in the future. But the socialism or communism they seek is a system created by and for the people of their continent. They want no imported pattern. The struggle for social justice, prosperity, and economic independence will continue to bring sharp conflict and change to South America. Much of this conflict and change will be violent, but it will be necessary. No continent can be healthy when ways of living that are hundreds of years apart separate some of the people from the others, and when millions live on the verge of starvation while a privileged few enjoy great luxury.

Although South America is very ancient, it is surprisingly new. It has a long history, and yet it is one of the great continents of the future. Today South Americans are looking to the possibilities of the years to come and are struggling to make their future a glorious one.

Index